MEMOIRS OF A
FUTURE GHOST

HEATHER SCARBRO DOBSON

Editor: Wayne South Smith, www.waynesouthsmith.com
Cover Designer: Lindsay Starr, www.lindsaystarr.com
Cover and Author Photographer: Paige Brigman,
    onelovephotography.zenfolio.com
Interior Designer: Jera Publishing, www.self-pub.net

ISBN: 978-1-7331601-0-0

DEDICATION

This book is dedicated to my male loved ones who
have passed on before me.

They believed in me, encouraged me, and loved me
even in the most difficult of times.

I miss them terribly but feel their presence every day.

My grandfather Simeon Berkley
My father Thomas Scarbro
My uncle Curtis Scarbro
My uncle Romie Scarbro

CONTENTS

FOREWORD
by Larry Flaxman

For as long as I can remember, I've been a seeker of truths. Knowledge of the forbidden, the hidden, and the arcane have always been of extreme interest to me. Throw in the element of mystery or conspiracy, and it's a recipe for my attention: ghosts, UFO's, Bigfoot, Elvis sightings, psychic phenomenon, the Loch Ness monster, time travel, who shot JFK?

If it was unexplained then it became a personal challenge to search for answers.

As a child, I can remember visiting the local libraries and spending hours lost in my own thoughts. I'd read, study, and take copious notes... all in the pursuit of knowledge. I simply had to understand.

In my young mind, I believed that the truths were all there. Perhaps hidden in plain sight... waiting for a true-to-life Indiana Jones to find. I wanted to be that individual.

Once I was old enough to drive I began to explore... often pushing the limits while venturing further and further beyond the artificially imposed geographic boundaries set by my parents. Always searching...

As I grew and matured—mentally, emotionally, and spiritually—I noticed a distinct pattern: order within the chaos. I realized that my research had organically taken on a more singular focus.

While still captivated by all things weird and unexplained, it had become clear that I had been on autopilot for many years... driven by the realization—and perhaps fear—of my own mortality.

As we are all too often made aware, we have but a short time before we shuffle off this mortal coil.

Of course, almost from birth, we are continually reminded of the solemn message that when you die there are but two possibilities: heaven or hell.

One is filled with fire, pain, and suffering. Banished to a horrific place where you are forced to live out eternity with strangers who have met similar fates.

The other is filled with joy, hope, love, and the belief that you will be reunited with loved ones who have passed over before.

But do we know this for sure? Is there any scientific proof—black and white—that either of those scenarios are conclusive?

Regardless of your belief, it can be inferred from these long-standing socio-religious tenets, that "something" happens after physical death of the human organism.

But that's the million-dollar question: "What?" There is an increasing amount of both anecdotal and experiential data that points to the possibility of what I like to call the "continuity of life."

Study a small sampling of the thousands of reported cases of near death experiences or reincarnation, and you will quickly gain a more profound belief that death is truly not the end.

My involvement in paranormal research stems from my own personal quest to discover undeniable scientific proof of the afterlife. Since the dawn of time, this evidence has eluded mankind. However, with the increasing availability and utilization of modern technology, I believe that we are moving in the proper direction.

From what we know of energy and matter, there are certain authoritative rules, which, according to our understanding of the physical world, cannot be broken. Utilizing modern technology, we can measure and quantify things which have been previously beyond our capability. One need only look to the groundbreaking research currently underway at the Large Hadron Collider (LHC) at CERN (European Organization for Nuclear Research) as proof that science has likewise taken on divergent beliefs.

When Heather asked me to write the foreword to her first book I was incredibly honored... and terrified. As a multiple bestselling author, I understand the importance of a powerful foreword, so, I'm humbled beyond words that she chose me to brand her very first entry into the shark-infested waters of literary publication.

I was also terrified because... well... I had absolutely no idea what the book was even about. I'm a science guy, and people typically consider me to be a skeptic. With a title such as *Memoirs of a Future Ghost*, I automatically assumed that the book would be rife with anecdotal fluff and pseudoscience. Was this another attempt to meld "fake science" with reality? Or would this book actually provide substantive answers?

Was it too late to politely decline?

Little did I know that I was in store for a real treat.

Initially I skimmed the chapters, but, found myself going back to fully read each one. And taking notes... lots of notes. There were so many parallels between our ideas and beliefs that it was uncanny. How the hell did she get inside of my head? This was most definitely not a half-baked attempt to reconcile known scientific tenets against new age drivel.

As I became more engrossed in the book, it became much more obvious that we have walked similar paths. Through her stories and experiences, it was obvious that Heather was a seeker too.

Memoirs of a Future Ghost is an eclectic tome full of literary wins. Heather's first endeavor offers interesting and unique perspectives on many paranormal topics. She has hit all the right buttons: ghosts, UFO's, Mothman, orbs... it's all here interspersed with empirical science tempered against agnostic beliefs. Throw in a healthy smattering of humorous undertones and you have a undeniable formula for success. This was one of those rare books which I simply couldn't put down.

If you are a searcher, you owe it to yourself to read this book cover to cover.

"It is the writer who might catch the imagination of young people, and plant a seed that will flower and come to fruition."
– Isaac Asimov

Larry Flaxman is a best-selling author, researcher, public speaker, and Co-Founder of the Bridge of Compassion Foundation. Visit www.LarryFlaxman.com

WHY I DO THIS

C harleston, West Virginia, was very cold on February 6, 1972. Thirty-two degrees Fahrenheit cold, in fact. It didn't snow that day, but it was a Sunday and I was born at 8:30 a.m., well before Oakhurst Presbyterian Church's Sunday service. My birth was announced before the service began, likely as an explanation as to my mother's absence from choir that morning. Oh, she sang, all right, just not any Christian hymns. My due date was six days prior, and I'm sure my parents, wondering when I was going to make my grand entrance into the world, were grateful that I finally decided to show up to the party, albeit fashionably late. In addition to being late, I was also a breach birth. My mother likes to constantly point out—to everyone—that she gave birth to me without benefit of localized anesthesia and that I had the gall to come out rear first in spite of that. We're both drama queens, it seems.

My first moments on this Earth pretty much sum up how I approach the world around me. I can be very hesitant, scared, and anxious of everything and everyone and I much prefer the sanctity of what I know versus the challenging unknown. I'm a hermit who would rather stay at home, order everything online, and wave to my neighbors from afar rather than actually get out there and do things and meet people. When

I reflect on this behavior and why I prefer safety over adventure, I know it stems from fear. My fear of living is rooted in death.

For as long as I can remember, I was terrified of death. Of course, all children are frightened by death. No child should ever be confronted with death, with no future, no possibility, no life. The first time I realized I would die, that my life would someday end, I was just a young girl, no more than five years old, and my parents and I had just returned from a visit to my grandparents' house in Lewisburg, West Virginia. My great-grandmother had just passed away, and it was my first brush with death. Standing in the funeral home, seeing all the adults around me crying, I couldn't understand why Little Mama wouldn't wake up. Finally, my cousin Stacey and I were allowed to lean up and look in the coffin. There, Little Mama lay so very peacefully, but her face looked drawn and too pale. My grandmother said I could touch her hand, which I did, only to discover that her hand was cold, stiff, and unyielding. I could no longer feel the blood moving beneath her skin, I couldn't see the flexing of her tendons. I glanced at her face, and she didn't flinch at my touch. I began to understand the concept of death and what happened to us, but the idea wasn't truly driven home until the next day when we processed to the cemetery. There, I watched as the cemetery workers began lowering Little Mama into the ground, and I was utterly horrified at the idea of spending forever, an eternity, in the ground.

My first night home in Charleston as I struggled to fall asleep, I tried to imagine forever, infinity, and I couldn't. I attempted to visualize my body as cold as Little Mama's, my parents crying over my casket, and what forever would be like in the cold, wet ground, and I couldn't. My mind locked up.

I shot up out of the bed, my chest heaving. I unwound my sheet from my legs and jumped from bed, ran into the living room where the soft glow from the TV shone like a beacon, and cried, "Mom! Dad! I'm going to die! Why am I going to die?" I honestly don't recall the ensuing conversation that night or on subsequent nights.

During the day, with the hustle and bustle of school and friends, I didn't have to think about death, but when the night crept in, the books were put away, and the TV turned off, my mind went to all the places it wasn't supposed to go, and I had no way of stopping it. Eventually, I could see the frustration in my parents' eyes, their inability to calm me down with platitudes about Heaven and God was evident, and so I lied. I told them that I was fine and that I was no longer scared of death or forever. Instead, I snuck books under my covers, along with an old flashlight, and read my fears away. Thanks to Nancy Drew, Judy Blume, and Sweet Valley High paperbacks, I avoided the worst of my fears with distraction. I would pick up my latest novel and delve into whatever story it wove, losing myself in its plot. Gradually, I learned how to insert myself into the story and act it out in my mind as I fell asleep. I became so good at this that it's still a tactic I use today. Like, in my mind it's not "Harry Potter." It's "Heather Potter," and I've killed Voldemort hundreds of times. After all of that, I was okay... for a while.

I was able to hold the anxiety at bay until I went to college and decided early on to study physics. I always thought that if I wanted to live in another country, I should learn the language. So I figured that if I'm going to live on Earth, the third planet from the Sun, in the Orion Spiral Arm of the Milky Way Galaxy, in the Local Group of the Virgo Supercluster of the Universe, I should learn the local language. That language is math with physics as the translator, and I loved it.

One day during my junior year, I was browsing through a bookstore at the Gainesville mall. Dahlonega, Georgia, the small town where my college was located, had one stoplight, one MacDonald's, and not much else to keep thousands of college students entertained. While most of my fellow Saints were out carousing at the Athens, Georgia, bars, I had my nose crammed into whatever paperbacks my meager allowance from home could afford. As my hands skimmed along the spines of the books in the Science section, my eyes fell on one titled *The First Three Minutes* by Steven Weinberg. I immediately snatched it off the shelf and greedily rifled through the pages. It was a book about the first three minutes of the universe, about the Big Bang and everything that happened in the ensuing 180 seconds. That may not seem like a long time, and when we're talking about the age of the universe, it's less than the blink of an eye, but so many things happened in those first three minutes that it left me spellbound. As a physics major and science nerd, this book appealed to me on so many levels. Clutching it to my chest, I glanced back at the shelf and saw another book, a perfect companion to the first: *The Last Three Minutes* by Paul Davies.

Well, heck, I thought. *If I've got the first three minutes, I'd better get the last three, too.*

And so, I found myself at the checkout, absent-mindedly pulling out my wallet while reading the back of Paul Davies's book. In it, he details the possible ways in which our universe may end: entropy or The Big Crunch. Neither sounded like a beach vacation, but I had to take it back to the dorm, read it, and know. After 21 years, I had thought about my death quite a bit, but I had never contemplated the death of the universe.

The First Three Minutes was an amazing book, and I tore through it within a few days. When I finally had a break from studying, I delved into *The Last Three Minutes* and… it was a disaster. It's a wonder that my roommates didn't report me to the RA and have me committed. It talked about entropy, or the gradual heat-death of the universe, when all the stars would burn out, making the universe a cold, lifeless place. Or, it posited, maybe the universe would collapse back in on itself, gravity pulling all the stars back inward to the center, resulting in a huge crunch of everything, kind of like a gigantic universe-wide black hole. Both possibilities were horrifying and my brain chewed on them every night.

Everything is either going to collapse in on itself or expand infinitely until entropy, and then how can we exist after death? Death isn't forever. How can death be forever if the universe isn't forever? We have to exist within the universe in some form or fashion. Energy can't be lost, so what's the point? Why even care? What's the point of anything? Why keep the

Mona Lisa in a museum? Why have children? Why try to travel to other planets? What's the point of it all?

Yeah. Junior year sucked. And unfortunately for Paul Davies, I chucked his book in the garbage can.

I managed to adapt and move on. With lots of studying, reading, and watching late-night 90s sitcoms in the dorm's lobby, I was able to distract my brain from all the speculating and wondering and calculating. *I don't have time for this! I have finals! And a life to live!*

But, the idea of my inevitable death, coupled with the deaths of mankind and the universe, always lounged in the back of my subconscious, waiting for the right moment to come out and toy with my anxieties. Eventually, I graduated with honors with my physics degree, spent a semester studying the behavior of ionized particles in Earth's polar magnetosphere, decided against a master's degree, and married my high school sweetheart.

When getting married in a traditional Christian service, two people promise to love each other in sickness and in health, in wealth and in poverty, until death separates them. My poor fiancé, now husband, Tyler, had no idea that he would also be tying himself to an anxiety-ridden nutcase who would randomly wake him up in the middle of the night and ask him to hold her through her death-induced panic attacks. We spent many nights watching old *Star Trek* episodes to calm me down, and just having that touch of another human being helped me immensely. Well, that and seeing a shirtless William Shatner! Many nights, I would slip out of our bed to watch TV in the living room, eventually falling asleep on the couch, all in a bid to keep from disturbing Tyler. One night, he informed me, "You don't bother me when you turn on the TV. I don't want you to be alone, and I don't want to be alone. Stay here."

Best. Husband. Ever.

And again, everything was fine for a while until we went and had kids.

I sometimes wonder if the sorority of pregnancy and motherhood includes a hazing ritual that embraces the notion of "let her figure it out on her own." I read just about every pregnancy book out there, and all of them told me how my back would hurt, how the baby would develop each day, that I would need to put my feet up from time to time, blah, blah… but absolutely none of them—and none of the women who took this gigantic step before me—told me about the postpartum night sweats that would leave my bed soaked. I wasn't informed of the cramping I would experience when breastfeeding, and I had no idea about the all-encompassing fear and panic that would overwhelm me.

My postpartum mental health transitioned from "I don't want to die!" to "I don't want *them* to die!!" Thankfully, my OB gave me a prescription for an anti-depressant, and within a few days, I was calmer, more focused, and less anxious. But the question still remained, would my children continue to exist after their inevitable end? And would there be an infinity waiting for them, even with the end of the universe a forgone conclusion? I absolutely *had* to know.

Unfortunately for me, faith wasn't something I had a lot of. This wasn't something to contemplate or stew on or take words from a holy book at face value and hope for the best. I absolutely, positively *had* to know. And I had to be able to tell my children, "Yes! I know for a fact that there is existence after death. I've seen it, felt it, and heard it. You will continue." And as a scientist I had to have that empirical evidence that life persisted after death.

Fortunately for me, there were like-minded individuals in the Atlanta-area, where Tyler and I settled, who were looking for the same answers and willing to allow me to tag along. It was 35 years into my journey on this Earth that I became a paranormal investigator, a person who wants to talk to ghosts, see them, have those chilling experiences that make me question life and the world around me. It took some persuasion from Tyler and some detective work on my end to even find a group here that investigated the paranormal, would be willing to take me on, and would be a group of people with whom I could work well. When I finally found them, not only did they help me find those answers, they also became a part of my family. I guess you could say that they've not only enriched my life, but my afterlife, as well.

Have I found the answers I seek? Yes. Have the panic attacks subsided? Absolutely. Am I still trying to scientifically prove that life exists after death? Definitely. Why? Because I want all of humanity to someday know, without a doubt, that they will never cease to exist. I know that may not happen in my lifetime or even in my children's, but I'm extraordinarily proud to be a part of building the foundation, knowing someday the work of paranormal investigators across the world will pay off.

So many people in this world are terrified of death. I find it odd that in a society steeped in faith and religion that seeks to answer those questions, that most people, when asked, will tell you they are afraid of death. Whether it's because of the idea of eternal punishment, the unknown, or our culture's tendency to leave death to the professionals—the clergy, and the funeral homes—I don't know. But, I've come to realize that only in facing death, understanding that it's inexorably bound to life, and that those who have gone before us are still around us, can we truly embrace it as a friend. Death isn't something to be feared. It is something to be respected, to help remind us of the joys of life. That's something I hope everyone comes to understand.

THE MOTHMAN

"**M**om! Dad! Can you take me to the library?" I would ask.

"Again?" would come the inevitable reply from either of my parents.

I would just shrug my shoulders, hold up the three or four books I had read in a week's time, and put on my best pitiful face. Of course, one or both of them would acquiesce and load me into our rust-bucket Honda Civic, and drive me to the squat, brick building on the corner of Fourth Avenue and D Street in downtown South Charleston. Sometimes they would follow me inside. Other times, my father would go across the street to skulk the halls of the Police Department or City Hall and visit with his friends and coworkers, leaving me to my own devices.

As I would walk up to the front of the South Charleston Public Library, a sense of calm would permeate my being. I would push open the heavy glass door, sneakers scuffing the concrete entrance way. My eyes would glance up at the announcements tacked to bulletin board, and I would swiftly walk to the second set of doors, leading me into the library itself. The crunch of the carpet and the overwhelming smell of paper and binding glue would envelop me like Aunt Clorine's hugs. Right there, across from the entrance, was the large circulation desk, where the stern-faced librarians would glance up from stacks of returned books, noting my entrance, and returning to their important work. I would take a sharp right and make my way to the children's section and their copious selection of Judy Blume, Roald Dahl, and Madeleine L'Engle. I would gleefully make my choices and take a seat in the small wooden chairs to read the first few chapters of each book. When finished, I would clutch the books tightly to my chest and reverently hand my card over to the librarian. Once home, the books never lasted very long, and it was only a matter of days before I was back at the corner of D Street and Fourth, selecting new books to fuel my addiction.

One day, though, I discovered that those preteen mysteries, romances, and sci-fi books were tiring with their predictable storylines and static characters. I wanted more. I wanted to be challenged, enlightened, and scared. Because of my voracious reading, the children's section, once abundant with books, had suddenly become woefully understocked.

There's nothing left, I thought. *Really?* Superfudge? *Read it.* Tales of a Fourth Grade Nothing? *Read that too.* Beverly Cleary's Dear Mr. Henshaw? *That's a book about a boy. Not interested. I've read the* Narnia *books three times already. I want to read about ghosts! That's what I want!*

Except, when it came to the paranormal genre, the only thing I could find was a collection of West Virginia folk tales about ghouls and mountain monsters. I didn't want stories; I wanted real ghosts. It was then that I made an important decision. I turned around and faced the vast, carpeted cavern separating the children's books from the adult fiction and nonfiction. Standing there, I stared at the bounty of books I had yet to discover and willed my legs to move. This first step, across the library where the adults wandered and perused titles, would be a difficult one. Finally, I took a deep breath and boldly strode across the void. Here, the shelves were taller, wider, and stocked with everything imaginable. There were mysteries with bloody knives dripping from the covers, science fiction featuring bold heroes and their futuristic spaceships, and the latest Jackie

Collins books to satisfy the housewives and their unsatisfactory lives. My fingers traced over the spines, looking for something, anything out of the ordinary. I made my way around the space and into a back corner, isolated from the rest of the large, open room. It was there I found odd tomes with titles that included the words "haunted" and "strange." My eyes were immediately drawn to one book in particular. It was a small hardback in a cream-colored dust jacket with a drawing of a winged creature with red eyes. I was awed and intrigued at the same time, and I absolutely couldn't put it down. This book, I knew, was going to be a game changer for me. When I finally pulled my eyes away from those red spots, I read the title: *The Mothman Prophecies*.

Wow! I thought prophecies only happened in the Bible! What the heck is this?

I began flipping through the book and saw words like "creature" and "bridge collapse" and "Men in Black" and I knew I had to take this home.

As I tentatively walked across the squeaky carpet toward the circulation desk, I imagined every eye turned toward me. I thought for sure that one of the many adults standing nearby would run over, snatch the book out of my hand, and tell me to get back to the children's section where I belonged. The loud carpet served only to draw attention to my plight, and as I handed the book and my library card to the imposing woman behind the counter, I was convinced that she would shake her head, tell me no, and guide me back to the monotony of the Hardy Boys and the Bobbsey Twins. But, to my surprise, she stamped the card with the due date and handed *The Mothman Prophecies* back to me without comment.

Now? The trick was to get it past my overprotective parents.

I blame my father for my interest in the paranormal. He would fill my head with tales of aliens, strange lights, coal mine ghosts, and tommy-knockers. Any strange story in the newspaper about Bigfoot or a TV news report about ghosts, and we would talk about the possibilities of other worlds and weird creatures.

At the end of each conversation, he would ask me, "Do you believe any of that is true? Because, I'm not sure."

"I don't know, Dad," I would reply, "but I hope it is true. All of it."

When I found *The Mothman Prophecies* and took it home, I thought that my parents may not approve, but I felt that if I showed it to my father first, I may have an ally.

I handed him the book, pointed out the cover, and asked him, "Daddy? Have you ever heard of the Mothman?"

"Yes! I have," he replied. He closely examined the cover. "Kind of creepy-looking, isn't he?"

I nodded and asked, "What is he?"

Dad responded, "I don't know. I remember reading the newspaper when it all happened, and none of them could decide if it was an alien or a sandhill crane." He shook his head with an air of disgust. "Those people knew what they were seeing, though. It wasn't some bird. It was a creature. And they were terrified."

He then regaled me with the parts of the story he could remember. It was one of jumpy teenagers, an old TNT storage area, and a West Virginia town in the grip of UFO fever and alien madness. It all started on November 15, 1966, when two young couples had driven out to the former WWII munitions storage area near Point Pleasant to do whatever it is young couples in cars like to do. When they first saw the creature, they were panic-stricken. It was large, grey, and shaped like a man with two legs and arms. The eyes, though, glowed a sinister red, and from its arms sprouted enormous wings. As the couples fled, the monster launched into the air and followed their car from above, even keeping up with them when their speedometer topped the scale. The local media immediately dubbed the beast "The Mothman," and a legend was born.

As the sightings increased over the next year, the townsfolk who inhabited this sleepy hamlet on the banks of the Ohio River wondered what kind of evil harbinger had invaded their quiet lives. Mary Hyre, a reporter for *The Athens Messenger* out of Ohio, managed the newspaper's sister office in downtown Point Pleasant. During the copious sightings, it was Mary who reported on the odd occurrences and the terror that gripped the community.

Eventually, the stories reached the attention of John Keel, a journalist, scriptwriter, and UFOlogist. At the time of the Mothman sightings, he wrote for *Flying Saucer Review* and understandably became curious about the reports of strange lights, visits from Men in Black—men dressed in black suits who would harass families who had witnessed the Mothman or the UFOs but who didn't seem normal because they acted very robotic, and no government agency would claim knowledge of them—and a grey creature with pulsing red eyes. He immediately connected with Mary, and the two began their months-long investigation of Mothman.

As the sightings increased and the mystery deepened, everything abruptly ended on December 15, 1967, when the Silver Bridge, the span that connected Point Pleasant to Gallipolis, Ohio, on the other side of the Ohio River, collapsed. Forty-six people died that day, and it was determined that a small 0.1-inch defect on the 13th steel pin eye-bar on the bridge, coupled with heavy Christmas traffic stalled on the bridge due to poorly-timed stoplights, contributed to the collapse of the forty-year-old, shoddily-maintained crossing. Yet, many people claim to have seen the Mothman on the bridge that day and still, fifty years later, blame it for the bridge's collapse.

I was absolutely enthralled.

"Daddy! Do you really think the Mothman caused the bridge to collapse? That's horrible!"

"I don't know, Ferntuck. But the people were absolutely terrified of him. Whatever he was, he was connected, somehow, to the bridge collapsing," he replied, shushing me because Mom had walked in and didn't like talk that may keep me up all night trying to avoid nightmares.

Later, as he tucked me in bed, he left me with a little nugget.

"Did you know there was another monster?" he asked.

I shook my head.

"It was the Braxton County Monster," he whispered, "and that guy showed up in 1952 when I was a Marine in Korea during the war. Don't know much about it, but he scared a bunch of people too!"

Of course, I stayed awake late into the night, imagining hairy monsters and flying creatures with red eyes, dreaming up all the ways I would try to communicate with the Mothman and tell it not to collapse the Silver Bridge again.

The world of 1967 Point Pleasant, West Virginia, was one of panic, confusion, and a distrust of the government. I saw the events of those 13 months through the eyes of John Keel and Mary Hyre and relived the tragic collapse of the Silver Bridge. Suffice it to say that my adolescent mind was blown, and I was sold on John Keel's conclusion that the Mothman was an ultraterrestrial, a creature of this world but of a different dimension, able to show itself to us as a warning but unable to communicate directly with humankind. It could only appear and use its menacing appearance to warn us of any harm to come. And that harm was 46 lives lost in the Ohio River.

What made the Mothman even more fascinating for me was that all of it took place in West Virginia some 50 miles from my bedroom. Now, there's nothing incredibly special about Point Pleasant, but what made it significant for me was that every year, my mother's family trekked there for our super-sized Berkley family reunion. The descendants of my great-grandfather, Thomas Joseph Berkley, met every Independence Day in Alderson, West Virginia, but in late August, those same cousins, as well as the descendants of my great-grandfather's siblings—Pearl, Alfred, Harvey, and Frederick—would all gather in Point Pleasant for an entire weekend of familial activities. What I recall most about those weekends were the sticky, August heat, the dusty baseball fields and rusty playgrounds, the huge quantities of food and playing with distant cousins until late into the night. As the sun set, we would sit, dirty and sticky, with our parents, and watch the communal bonfire, listening to the "pickin' and grinnin'" of Berkley cousins who played their banjos, mandolins, and washtub basses. I remember one year in particular when Cousin Ocalla's luggage was raided and next morning we found her extremely large bra had been run up the flagpole. If any symbol could perfectly embody the fun-loving Berkley family, it was a triple-D brassiere, flapping high in the morning breeze. Good times.

During the early years of my childhood, I would ride in the back of my parents' Honda Civic with the windows down, watching the changing landscape between Charleston and Point Pleasant. As we neared the reunion campground, the mountains gave way to a wide valley of picturesque farms and a lazy Kanawha River. In the immediate years after reading *The Mothman Prophecies*, I would begin to imagine the Mothman peering out at us from between the distant trees. I wondered where his hiding places could be when he watched our family reunion. Was he just outside the range of our bonfire or perched above us in the treetops? I wondered if he watched us out of curiosity or in anger. When the sun would start to go down and the bonfire would burn bright, I made sure to stay as far away from the tree line as possible because even though I was curious, I wasn't crazy. I wanted to be the last one to be mesmerized by those glowing, red eyes so that I could run far away. Hey, I may have fantasized about communicating with the Mothman, but when the chips were down, I knew I was just a kid who needed to run fast and not try to save the day!

The summer after reading John Keel's book, I was a very precocious ten-year-old. That year, instead of going with my parents, I rode with my grandparents to the reunion. We arrived a day early and stayed in a local Point Pleasant hotel. As usual, I had a hard time falling asleep because it was a strange bed, a strange place, and I was sharing a bed with my cousin Stacey. As an only child, I was used to sharing my bed with only my collection of still, stuffed animals. Stacey was neither still nor stuffed. But there was something else looming in the back of my mind.

This was Point Pleasant. The Mothman was near. I could feel it.

I eventually fell asleep in the fading dusk only to wake up a few hours later. As I slowly opened my eyes, confused by the strange feel of the unfamiliar blanket covering me, I immediately became alert when I looked to the foot of the bed. In the dim light coming from under the door, I saw him. The Mothman. He was silently standing at the foot of our bed, watching us. I blinked my eyes, willing my blurry vision away. I thought to reach for my glasses, but I knew that if I moved, the Mothman would attack. As I lay in that bed, the light from the hallway continued to illuminate the room and the immovable figure that stood guard between me and freedom. I was terrified. I lay there utterly frozen in fear. Stacey was only inches away, but she wouldn't be able to help much in a fight. I was a scrawny kid, and she was even smaller than me. My strong, wiry Paw-Paw soundly slept just a few feet away, and even though I knew that manhandling cattle and plowing fields gave him the strength to take on the giant figure watching us, I knew the second I got out of the bed, the Mothman would have me.

And so, I stayed there for the rest of the night, wide awake, trying to control my panicked breathing and not taking my eyes off the imposing figure. If it could be absolutely still, then so could I. I spent what seemed like hours counting each heartbeat and making sure I didn't move or make a sound. Finally, as the room lightened from the rising sun, I felt a sense of relief because I knew my agony would soon pass. Paw-Paw and Grandma would wake up and chase the Mothman away.

As the sun rose, I could more clearly see Stacey and my grandparents. The birds outside began chirping, my surroundings became brighter, and I realized that what I had feared all through that dark night was… a coat tree. In my abject terror, I forgot about its presence across from our bed, and in the dim light with my poor, near-sighted vision, the once-slender coat tree took on thick, menacing proportions. I was doubly thankful that not only had the Mothman avoided our hotel room, but that I also hadn't woken my grandparents to protect me from a misidentified piece of furniture.

A short time later, my grandmother shook Stacey awake, and we made ready to check out and leave for the reunion. I was exhausted, elated, hungry, and crashing from an all-night adrenaline rush. Even though I normally shared everything with Stacey, I didn't utter a word about my sleepless night to her, and when I finally saw my parents later that day, I mumbled to my father that the day and night before were boring and uneventful. In order to save face, I knew I couldn't mention a word of that long night to anyone. And until now, I never did.

THE BRAXTON
COUNTY MONSTER

When I brought home John Keel's *The Mothman Prophecies*, it was as if the floodgates had opened. My father started telling me every West Virginia legend he could remember. One of those was of the Braxton County Monster. He was rather vague in the telling, giving me scant information about a group of children and adults who saw this... thing somewhere in Braxton County in the 1950s. It was understandable that he wasn't sure of the exact story because when the Braxton County Monster was terrorizing residents of Flatwoods, West Virginia, my father had been drafted into the Marine Corps and was serving in Posang, Korea. I didn't know what the monster looked like, if it had been seen since, or where it could be hiding. So, of course, my 10-year-old brain filled in the blanks.

For me, the Braxton County Monster was just another version of Bigfoot: tall, hairy and, I assumed, roaming the forest at night terrorizing the locals. I stewed on what I knew, and when I returned *The Mothman Prophecies* to the library, thoroughly terrified and thrilled, I went looking for a book about the Braxton County Monster. The only problem was there was no such thing. People I asked had no clue what I was talking about. I returned home and asked Dad where he had heard the story, and he recalled that it was, again, from letters sent to him in Korea from his mother. I was disappointed and went back into my room to delve into a book about the funerary practices of ancient man. Since I couldn't find a book on the Braxton County Monster, I instead settled on a book in which the illustration of a Neanderthal burial caught my attention. The woman had been bound into a fetal position, painted with red ochre—representing blood—and placed in a shallow grave in a cave. I loved the idea of death being a rebirth into the afterlife, and I decided right then that I would like to be buried in this manner. The only problem was I couldn't figure out how to broach the subject with my parents.

Yes, I had issues.

Two years later, I was a cynical 12-year-old and very active in the Girl Scouts. During every regular meeting, I fidgeted and scratched and fought against my ill-fitting Girl-Scout-green jumper and my scratchy wool socks. Girl Scout uniforms were in no way flattering and I didn't care how many adults said I was cute, I despised those stupid little orange tassels that stuck out from the sides of my socks. As I sat and picked at those horrendous things, our troop leader attempted to gain our attention.

"Girls! GIRLS! I have very exciting news! We are going camping!"

The collective groan from the assembled group was appropriately loud.

"Now, now!" our troop leader rejoined, "calm down! It will be fun! We're going to have the opportunity to earn badges, and hike, and…"

The groans were even louder now. Except from me. My interest was piqued. Badges? Did she say badges? I looked down at my sash, resplendent with numerous pins and badges. Those small round pieces of fabric filled the bottom half of my sash front and were slowly climbing the back. I was the type of kid that could be bribed with sparkly trophies, medals, pins, and badges. The more, the better, as far as I was concerned.

And any opportunity to weigh my thin, green sash down with more thread and pepperoni-sized badges was an opportunity that I relished.

The troop leader was still nattering on, now trying to convince all the girls that this trip was going to be worth it because of campfires! And s'mores! But she already had me at badges. My mouth watered at the thought of another completed row.

And then? She burst my bubble when she announced, "We'll take a quick bus ride to the lodge in Braxton County, just north of here."

In my thoughts, I questioned, *Braxton County? The Braxton County? As in the home of the Braxton County Monster? Nuh-uh. Not going. Forget it.*

"The Mothman Debacle"—what I liked to call my night of terror at the hands of a hotel coat tree simply because that name made it sound dramatic and important rather than what it really was—reminded me that although I had escaped death at the hands of one West Virginia monster, there were more out there. There was a reason Chris Carter set many episodes of *The X-Files* in West Virginia. It's a beautiful place, full of strange lights, creature sightings, and stories of vengeful ghosts. I had to keep my guard up and make sure I stayed safe in the capital city of Charleston where the worst that could happen to me was a whiff of rotten eggs from the local chemical plant. There was no way I was going to be witness to a horrible monster mowing its way through a group of hapless Girl Scouts, me included. I remember feeling sick to my stomach and wanting to break every bone in my body so that I could avoid this trip, but I couldn't. Badges be damned, my life wasn't worth a few pieces of fabric. Except, I was trapped in the same conundrum every kid finds herself in when dealing with fears and parents. I could already hear the failed conversation with my parents.

"Moooo-oooom! I can't go on this trip! It's too dangerous! What about the Braxton County Monster?!" I would beg.

"What?! What are you talking about? A monster? There's no such thing!" she would respond.

And then, I would stamp my feet. "I'm not going anywhere near Braxton County because of the monster that lives there! Dad told me all about it!"

Mom would most likely holler at my Dad from the kitchen. "Tom Scarbro! Get in here! What have you told Heather about this Braxton County Monster?"

My father would most likely throw up his hands and mumble, "Aw, hell, Jo. She asked me about the Mothman, so I told her about it. And then, she asked me about other weird West Virginia stuff, so I had to tell her."

Mom would then throw up her hands, exasperated, and declare, "Well, she's going! I've already paid! She's earning badges! We just bought her a new canteen! And stop scaring her!"

Dad would shuffle off, defeated, until he was out of Mom's line of sight when he would look back at me and smile and wink, and we would both know that he wouldn't stop scaring the snot out of me because I would keep asking for him to do just that. And, let's face it, I was Daddy's little girl. He couldn't give me the moon, so he gave me monsters instead.

I would turn to Mom, sigh, and acquiesce. "Fiiiii-iiine. I'll go. But if I end up dead in the woods because the Monster killed me, it'll be all your fault!" And then I'd flounce out of the kitchen.

I just didn't want to go through all of that. So instead, I kept my mouth shut, got on a bus, and kept my eyes glued to the windows. The interstate outside of Charleston gave way to the two-lane curvy roads of backwoods West Virginia. As I kept my focus on the roadside for the "Braxton County" sign, I had to fight off my seat mate—who incessantly talked—and our troop leader who wanted us to sing *Make New Friends* in a round for the 50th time. Eventually, the sign came into view, and my attention was immediately riveted to the trees lining the roadside. I kept my eyes open for any hint of a giant, furry beast.

Finally, we arrived at the camping lodge and divvied up the bunk beds. I took a top bunk, not only because I liked privacy, but also because maybe the monster would go for the easier, low-hanging fruits of the girls in the lower beds. I pulled my blanket over my head and fitfully slept.

The next day was full of singing, craft-making, cooking over open fires, and a long hike through the woods. I was fine until we left the lodge. In addition to my canteen, I packed my Swiss Army pocket knife. I decided that even though my puny knife wouldn't harm a chipmunk, I wouldn't go down without a fight. I was going to gut whatever came upon us in the woods, and if I wasn't successful, my parents would just have to stand beside my grave, Mom clutching my bloodied pocket knife, staring down at my naked body, tied into a fetal position, covered in red ochre, while I looked down from above, shaking my head and shouting, "Told you!"

The hike began innocuously enough. We were told to get out our compasses and to follow the troop leader's headings and directions. This was for a badge, so, of course, I paid close attention, but I also wanted fair warning of the Braxton County Monster sneaking up on us. While our leader prattled on about identifying poison ivy, which way was north, and how to identify animal tracks, I hiked along, listening to the sounds coming from the forest. Every snap of a branch, every rustle of leaves, I immediately zoned in to the direction from which the noise came. I was a highly paranoid 12-year-old, hopped up on adrenaline, waiting to shank any hairy monster that crashed through the trees. Three hours later, we arrived back to the lodge, hot, sweaty, and tired. Meanwhile, I was a mix of relieved and disappointed. Relieved that I didn't have to get bloody but disgruntled that I didn't get to see the infamous monster.

I couldn't wait to get on that bus the next morning and wave goodbye to Braxton County for the final time. I was proud that I had lived to tell the tale, but I was mostly happy that I didn't wail to my parents about my fears. Trying to recover from that embarrassment would be far worse than death. I vowed to myself that I would never again step foot in Braxton County, and I upheld that vow except for the few times we had to drive through on Interstate 79 to make our way north to Morgantown for the odd WVU Mountaineers football game.

Years later during a visit with Mom, we were at the local South Charleston arts and crafts fair and there, amongst the knit toilet paper roll covers and the handmade baby blankets, stood Frank Feschino, Jr. He was a tall, lanky man in his early 50s, a thick mop of black hair on his head and a generous mustache. His Connecticut accent let me know that he wasn't a local. His table displayed a stack of books, written by him, and the title was prominently displayed on the tablecloth: *The Braxton County Monster: The Cover-Up of the Flatwoods Monster Revealed.*

I was immediately drawn to him, and as I waited to speak to Mr. Feschino, I examined the book's cover art and what I noticed was the lack of fur on this monster. I realized it was less furry and more… alien. What I was looking at was an extraterrestrial, or a robot, or a combination of the two. I was dumbfounded. When Mr. Feschino was finished talking to the fair patron in front of me, I introduced myself and began to pepper him with questions.

"Hi! My name is Heather! So… the Braxton County Monster wasn't a Bigfoot?"

"No! Not at all!" he eagerly replied, animatedly gesturing toward the book cover. "It was all part of a UFO flap going on along the East coast in the early 1950s! The US government had ordered their military to shoot down any UFOs spotted over government installations. It was a real problem! And the Braxton County Monster was part of those sightings. It was a close encounter with an alien!"

He seemed excited to talk with someone who was generally interested in the subject. I just stood there with my mouth open.

"Wow!" I responded. "My father told me about the monster, but he didn't have all the details because he was out of the country in 1952, and I couldn't find any books on the subject in the library. I just assumed that the Braxton County Monster was a Sasquatch."

"Oh, no!" he exclaimed, handing me a copy of the book. "This wasn't anything like a Bigfoot! This was an alien!"

When I heard alien, I handed him every last bit of cash in my purse in exchange for a copy of his book. He happily signed it for me, and as I walked away, my mother chattering on about hand-knit washcloths on sale, five for three dollars, I immediately opened the book and stepped back into 1952 rural West Virginia. As my mother drove us home, I kept turning pages. As we ate dinner, I continued to read and stayed up late into the night, nose glued inside the book.

It turns out that my childhood imagination, without all of the pertinent information, had filled in the blanks and given rise to a monster that didn't exist. The story of the Braxton County Monster goes something like this. Three boys from Flatwoods, West Virginia, ranging in age from 10 to 13, saw a bright object fly across the sky on the evening of September 12, 1952. They saw the object come to rest on the property of a local farmer. Two of the boys, brothers, went home to tell their mother, Kathleen, about what they saw. Kathleen then set out with two other local boys and a 17-year-old West Virginia National Guardsman named Eugene Lemon, and his dog, to the farm where the UFO had landed. The dog ran ahead of them and quickly returned, tail between its legs, terrified. When the group reached the property, they witnessed a ball of fire and smelled something that made their noses and eyes burn. Eugene noticed smaller lights to the left of the fiery object and shined his flashlight in that direction. That's when the group saw the seven-foot tall creature. It had a black body with a luminous face and the body was described both as an exoskeleton and a metal suit. The eyes were glowing red, and the head was huge. It began moving toward them, making a high-pitched hissing noise. The group, of course, quickly ran home. After this, several members of the group fell ill. The symptoms they described were swollen throats and nasal irritation. Eugene suffered from vomiting and convulsions that night, and a local doctor who treated the sick members of the group stated their symptoms were similar to those of victims of mustard gas exposure.

Many have said that the Flatwoods group mistakenly identified a meteor, an aircraft hazard beacon, or a barn owl, and that they suffered from the physical effects of hysteria. But, why would a group of people lie about something that would only bring them eventual ridicule?

West Virginia has always been a place of contradiction. To the world, we're just a backwards land, full of uneducated, moonshine-drinking hillbillies. To those of us who were born and raised there, it's a beautiful place of mountains, fresh air, and friendly people who are fierce, loving, and kind. They may view strangers with suspicion but will give you anything you need if you only ask. It's a place of common sense mixed up with a healthy dose of superstition. Our early forefathers brought with them legends from across the Atlantic and combined them with local native stories. It's easy to think that the Braxton County Monster was born from those stories told to West Virginia's children, but I think we would be wrong in that assumption. Something happened on September 12, 1952, that can't easily be explained, and until I can go back in time to that night and experience the events myself, I'll trust Kathleen and Eugene and their story of an alien that crash-landed in the backwoods of Flatwoods, Braxton County, West Virginia.

I have no explanation for any of it, but what I do know is that I had rediscovered a monster of my youth, a monster that once roamed the land of Braxton County, West Virginia, for one night, twenty years before my birth and then disappeared without a trace. All of my worry and fear during my weekend Girl Scout excursion was for naught. Rather than combing the woods for a hairy creature, I should have scanned the skies for an alien craft. Problem is, there isn't a Girl Scout badge for that.

THE GREENBRIER GHOST

During my first twelve years, you could find me every summer, most holidays, and the odd long weekend in Lewisburg, West Virginia, at my grandparents' farm. My Paw-Paw Berkley had worked his entire adult life for C&P Telephone and had retired in his 60s. He and my Grandmother, also a C&P retiree, pooled their money in the early 1970s and bought a beautiful slice of land in the Greenbrier Valley. They called it Pleasant View Farm. At over 70 acres, it easily housed a small herd of Hereford cattle, a large garden, and three precocious grandchildren. Each morning, the fog rising from the Greenbrier River would blanket the fields and Paw-Paw's cows would appear like shadows through the mist. Cawing crows fluttered around the corn stalks in the garden next to the house, and we three girls—my cousins Weslea, Stacey, and I—could be found either roller-skating in the huge basement, rambling through the woods, or swinging on an old tire at the edge of the pasture. All three of us learned to drive at the wheel of Paw-Paw's trusty John Deere tractor, helped bale hay at the end of each summer, and shelled peas and shucked corn like we were trying to win a blue ribbon at the state fair. Most days, our grandparents would have to chase us out of Grandma's prized rose garden and shoo us off the blueberry bushes, our fingers stained dark purple. Paw-Paw had allowed us girls to tame one of the calves, and we named it Lollipop. He was a cute little Hereford that would come to us when called and lay docilely, waiting for scratches and attention. It wasn't until he grew into a large half-ton bull, leaning on us while munching on a pail of grain, that we all realized taming a calf wasn't such a great idea. That didn't stop us, though, from eventually naming two more cows Popsicle and Pickle and doing it all over again. Those first twelve years of my life were idyllic.

The route to Paw-Paw's and Grandma's was a long, two-hour drive over the twisting, winding Midland Trail. The section of I-64 between Beckley and Lewisburg had not yet been finished, and the Midland Trail was the most direct route to Lewisburg from Charleston. I would settle into the back seat of the baby blue Honda Civic, windows down in the summer, a bottle of Sunkist clutched tightly in my hands with my latest find from the library open on my lap. Within 30 minutes, I would inevitably fall asleep, waking up intermittently to take in the sights, but succumbing yet again to the deep, sweaty slumber that would prevent me from suffering the inevitable car sickness due to the winding roads. We would pass through towns like Belle, Glen Ferris, Rainelle, and Charmco. Gauley and Big Sewell Mountains would take us high into the sky, giving us beautiful vistas and hairpin turns. There were waterfalls, little towns that passed by in the blink of an eye, and the famous "Mystery Hole" where a quonset hut sat on the side of the road outside Ansted, a VW Beetle crashed into its side. Painted in bright colors it boasted the opportunity for passersby to "See the Laws of Gravity Defied!" We never stopped, and I'm still bitter about it to this day.

As we neared the end of the Midland Trail and could hop on the part of I-64 that was finished a few miles outside Lewisburg, we would pass through a town called Sam Black Church. On the side of the road was a historical marker that I practically memorized because it marked our nearness to summer fun on the farm:

Interred in nearby cemetery is Zona Heaster Shue. Her death in 1897 was presumed natural until her spirit appeared to her mother to describe how she was killed by her husband Edward [sic]. Autopsy on the exhumed body verified the apparition's account. Edward, found guilty of murder, was sentenced to the state prison. Only known case in which testimony from ghost helped convict a murderer.

"Daddy," I would ask, "what actually happened to that lady?"

"What lady?" he would reply, turning the steering wheel to guide us onto the interstate.

"The story on the sign." I pointed back toward the historical marker.

"Oh!" he briefly looked behind us and turned back to face the road. "I have no idea, Ferntuck. You'll have to look it up at the library when we get home."

And that's just what I did. Except I wasn't able to find any information. What I did find was a book called, *The Telltale Lilac Bush and Other West Virginia Ghost Tales*. It was a book of West Virginia ghostly folk tales, stories of murder, ghostly children, omens, coal mine spirits, and of course, death. These weren't just stories told to scare one another around the fire; these were stories to remind the isolated people of the Mountain State that death and danger were just around every corner.

The story for which the book was named caught my attention. It was about a husband and wife who lived along the Tygart Valley River in the northern part of the state. Their marriage wasn't happy, and one day, the wife disappeared. Neighbors noticed that upon her disappearance, the husband began to live it up with parties and much merriment. During one of these parties, a few of the attendees standing on the old man's front porch noticed a lilac bush next to the house, beating on the windowpane. On this windless night, the bush flapped back and forth as if beckoning them toward it. The party goers decided something was wrong and, against the old man's protests, decided to dig up the lilac bush. There, underneath, they found that the roots of the bush were growing from the palm of a woman's hand—the wife's hand. The old man screamed, ran off toward the Tygart, and was never seen again.

In my young mind, without knowing the true story of Zona Heaster Shue, I filled in the holes with *The Telltale Lilac Bush*, creating a new truth. And that truth was that at my grandparents' house was a bush growing outside the guest bedroom window, and it would brush against the window at the slightest wind. My grandparents lived in Greenbrier County; Zona had lived in Greenbrier County. *The Telltale Lilac Bush* was written by a West Virginia author. Maybe she was mistaken regarding the location of the lilac bush. I decided right then and there that Zona was under that bush at my grandparents' house. I didn't know how she got there, and I didn't care. No way was I sleeping in there at night. My parents could have that room and deal with the sound of that bush scraping against the window, beckoning them to dig it up and reveal her secret each night. I would spend my nights a mile away at my cousins' house. Their bedroom was on the second floor, and their windows were vegetation-free. Of course, they were also down the hill from the Greenbrier Memorial Gardens. But, I was strangely fine with that fact probably because they had a cool tree house and their neighbor had a swimming pool.

But, every day we were back at the farm. The basement was our hideaway, our clubhouse, our special domain. Under the stairs were shelves holding jars full of canned vegetables, fruits, and jams. In the center were old cabinets, chairs, and a quilt rack holding Grandma's latest project. Along one wall were shelves full of farming books and photo albums, and scattered about here and there were old boxes full of quilting scraps, costume jewelry, old shoes, clothes, and holiday decorations. As we three girls zoomed around the basement, the pom poms on our skates holding on for dear life, a constant whirring sound from our plastic wheels filled the air, and we would talk about so many things.

"Stacey!" I shouted over the clanking and humming. "What play should we do for the grown-ups?"

"Let's do one about Indian princesses!" she replied.

"We can dress up in Grandma's fabric!" shouted Weslea, turning the corner around a support pole at the far end of the basement where the dreaded "central vacuum monster" resided.

"And her jewelry!" Stacey added.

"Can I carry the walking stick?" I begged.

And the plans for a dramatic one-act play about a brave Native American princess and her tribe began to take form, all while we continued to circle the basement on our skates. Upstairs, we could hear our mothers, grandmother, and aunt in the kitchen. As they peeled fruit, cut up vegetables, and boiled jars and lids, they talked, bickered, and gave directions to one another.

Suddenly, the lights in the basement went off. The air vibrated with our screams and squeals as Uncle Larry growled and snarled. We took off to the far side of the basement and he tore down the stairs, giving chase. Just as he reached us, Aunt Joy hollered from upstairs.

"Larry Jones! You better not be scaring those girls!"

We giggled, and Uncle Larry innocently replied, "Of course not!"

The stairwell would be quiet for a moment and then Aunt Joy would retreat back upstairs, closing the door. This was our cue to act like idiots, howling, laughing, and chasing each other until none of us could breathe from the fierce tickle battle that ensued.

Those days at Pleasant View farm were my favorites, even with the imagined ghostly presence outside the guest bedroom window. What I didn't know at the time was that even though Zona Shue was long gone, there *was* something of a ghostly presence surrounding our lives. It was the ghosts of resentment wafting around us in the simmering steam, family strife coming to a boil, and mental illness sealed tightly in sterile jars that sat on a high shelf just over our little heads.

But, we'll come back to that.

Eventually, long after I grew up and moved to Georgia, I learned of the story of Zona Shue. In October, 1896, against the wishes of her mother, she married a blacksmith named Erasmus Stribbling Trout Shue.

Just give yourself a second and revel in how amazing that name is. I'm still bitter that I didn't give that name to one of my kids. Could you imagine shouting it? *"Erasmus Stribbling Trout Dobson! You get up here and pick up your dirty clothes, or you're in big trouble, mister!"* I missed out on a golden opportunity.

Anyway, back to poor Zona. She and Erasmus got along just fine until three short months later in January, 1897, when she was found dead at the foot of the stairs of her home, stretched out on her back with her feet together and one hand on her stomach. The boy who discovered her ran to tell his mother who then summoned the local doctor who was also the coroner. It took him an hour to arrive. In the meantime, Erasmus had arrived. He carried Zona upstairs, placed her on the bed, and dressed her in a high-necked dress with a veil over her head. When the doctor arrived, Erasmus stood at her head, clutching her and crying, becoming hysterical any time the doctor came near her head during his examination. Through the lace of the dress's high neckline, the doctor noted some bruising on Zona's neck, but concluded that she had probably died of "everlasting faint."

But, not all was as it seemed. Erasmus wouldn't let anyone go too near the coffin during the wake, and he had tied a scarf around Zona's neck, claiming it was her favorite. He vacillated between fits of crying and upbeat energy. Funeral-goers noticed that while being carried to the cemetery, Zona's head seemed to move easily from side to side. Mary Heaster, Zona's mother, was convinced that Erasmus had killed her daughter, and began praying every night for an answer.

Four weeks after the funeral, Mary Heaster was visited by her daughter's ghost on four separate nights and told her the same story each night. Zona told her that Erasmus had killed her because he thought she hadn't cooked meat for dinner. Zona said he had abused her, and on the night he killed her, he snapped her neck. To prove this, her ghost turned her head until it was facing backwards.

Of course, Mary Heaster was beside herself. She immediately reported the visitations to the local prosecutor who then re-opened the case and re-interviewed many of the interested and involved parties. Because the doctor admitted that he hadn't been able to perform a full examination, the prosector felt that an exhumation and autopsy were warranted. And so, a month after her death, Zona was exhumed and her autopsy lasted for three days. According to the report:

> The discovery was made that the neck was broken and the windpipe mashed. On the throat were the marks of fingers indicating that she had been choked. The neck was dislocated between the first and second vertebrae. The ligaments were torn and ruptured. The windpipe had been crushed at a point in front of the neck.

Of course, Erasmus was immediately arrested and tried for murder. Prosecutors later found out that he had been married twice before. He divorced his first wife who claimed that Erasmus had horribly abused her. His second wife died under mysterious circumstances less than a year after they were married. Zona, it seemed, had suffered the same fate. Erasmus was sent to the Moundsville Penitentiary for a life term, but died three years later from a mystery epidemic that swept through the prison. Zona's ghost never again visited her mother, and she was buried in the Soule Chapel Methodist Cemetery near the little town of Sam Black Church.

As a kid imagining that Zona still hovered over the Greenbrier Valley, influencing the movement of the bush outside my grandparents' house, what I didn't see was the discord looming over our family, waiting to impact all of our lives. What I missed while swinging on the tire, hiking in the woods, roller-skating in the basement, was my mother slowly but surely splitting from her family, ruining our happy moments with false accusations and lies. It all came to a head during Christmas, 1984, and when we left Lewisburg after that holiday, I had no idea I wouldn't return for another four years.

My visits with my grandparents became sporadic and then eventually nonexistent. My Paw-Paw was diagnosed with prostate and bone cancers. I was able to visit him before he died, but he probably had no idea I was there thanks to his morphine drip. He died in March, 1992. My cousins Weslea and Stacey grew up, married, and had children of their own. We never had any more childhood roller-skating sessions in the basement. My Aunt Joy died from skin cancer in April, 1995, one month before my wedding, and my Uncle Larry eventually re-married. These and so many other life events happened, and I wasn't there for them. I missed reunions, births, deaths, holidays, and so many moments.

Just recently, I reestablished contact with all of my Lewisburg loved ones. My Grandma still lives at Pleasant View Farm and welcomed me with open arms, reminding me that none of what had transpired was my fault. As I walked alongside the field one morning, devoid of the cattle my Paw-Paw had once cared for, I realized I had become the Greenbrier Ghost. In my absence, the lives of my extended family had gone on without me, and even though my life had continued, I was haunted by what had happened. The pictures of me in my grandparents' house are old; they are school pictures from the 80s and reflect a life that was. To this day, the question of what could have been saddens me, and as I continue to deal with the fallout, I will catch myself during each visit back to Pleasant View Farm running my hands over the old jewelry boxes we used to dig through as kids. My legs constantly take me down to the basement, the sounds of roller skates on the concrete just beyond my hearing. My hands flip through old, yellowing photo albums, tracing the faces of those who once were. And each time I'm there, I wish the bush outside the window would haunt me instead of the sad remembrance of a family interrupted.

HIGHER EDUCATION

My junior high years were an absolute dream. I had friends, good grades, and everything was swimmingly wonderful. And then? The fickleness of friends hit, and high school dawned cold and bleak. Friends I had cherished and thought would stand by me through thick and thin suddenly jumped ship and left me absolutely alone. Tenth grade arrived, and it was a year I would never wish to repeat. Even though I eventually made new friends who supported me and nourished my spirit, I was ready to say goodbye to the pain. As my time at South Charleston High School came to an end, I researched out-of-state colleges with physics programs. I wanted to get as far away from my home state as the student loans would allow and make a fresh start where no one knew me. When I walked across the stage of the Charleston Municipal Auditorium on a steamy June evening in 1990, I was ecstatic. I was more than ready for the adventure of college.

North Georgia College, in the very sleepy town of Dahlonega was everything I'd ever hoped it would be, except I was a little bit lonely. Five-hundred miles away from my parents, the landscape may have seemed familiar with the Blue Ridge foothills standing in for my beloved Appalachian Mountains, but everything was different. The accents weren't the same, and I learned to spend a lot of time alone. At first, I thought I would study medicine, having always loved the idea that I could help people and solve mysteries at the same time, but I realized early on that my heart was too soft and the loss of a patient would destroy me. Instead, I chose the completely cerebral studies of physics and math. My fellow physics majors were all male, and even though I had a roommate, we weren't exactly compatible. When sorority rush began in January of my first year, I knew that I should have signed up to participate. I had been active in the International Order of the Rainbow for Girls, a Masonic-affiliated group for girls between the ages of 12 and 20, and I craved a similar experience during my college years. There were no Rainbow Girl assemblies nearby, so I figured a sorority would be the next best thing. I vowed to join in during the next year's rush and, in the meantime, make friends with the girls from all the sororities so that when the time came to choose, it would be an easy decision.

My freshman year passed quietly until one night, during the winter quarter, when the girls on my hall decided it was a good night to scare each other with ghost stories. I, like all the other girls, had heard of the ghostly goings on in Lewis Hall, the freshman women's dorm where we lived. The apocryphal story went that a first-year girl had hung herself in her room on the fourth floor, the same floor I was living on.

C'mon, I thought. *What American college campus doesn't have a similar story? Someone killed themselves here. Someone else died of heartache here. Oh, look! Another woman in white! Of course, a ghost that's crying! It's just the same nonsense repeated over and over, perpetuated by the older generation trying to scare the young'uns. Somebody had to have invented this nonsense just to scare everybody.* I followed up my internal monologue with lots of eye rolling.

Not to say these stories aren't true, but they are never verifiable. Girls had claimed for years that that particular fourth floor room at the end of the hall was colder than the others, that they had seen a girl wandering the halls in just her nightgown, and that she could walk through the walls.

And it wasn't just Lewis Hall that received the ghostly treatment. Sanford dorm was supposedly haunted by Gretchen, a female member of the Blue Ridge Rifles, killed in a car accident. She was fond of pulling the covers off girls while they slept. Barnes Hall, an administrative building that once served as the original dining hall, was riddled with the sounds of rattling plates and flatware each night when the lights were turned off. Tyler, also a student at North Georgia, recounts doors closing on their own in the military dorms but attributes that to air pressure and wild imaginations.

Those same wild teen imaginations hit the fourth floor of Lewis Hall. So, on that cold, winter night, the story of the student who had hung herself made the rounds. We were all in our pajamas, ready for the day to end, staying inside rather than wandering campus because of the dropping temperatures. As the evening wore on and the story passed from room to room, it changed and morphed as it moved from girl to girl. Like the game "Telephone," the story was completely different by the time it spread through the entire floor. The adrenaline and anxiety built and built, and the moment it peaked, the fan at the end of the hall came on.

Now, these fans weren't the cheap, small fans you buy at Wal-Mart. These were huge fans installed at the end of each hall on each floor used to circulate air since Lewis was the only un-air conditioned building on campus. The rub, though, was these fans only turned on when the temperature was hot. They didn't activate in the colder temperatures like that evening.

When that fan came on, every girl nearby froze. Heads peaked out from doors, some with toothbrushes hanging out of their mouths, others in mid-crunch or mid-slurp, popcorn bags and cups held loosely in their hands, forgotten. Within a millisecond, the screams began. It started with the girls in the rooms closest to the fan in question and traveled down the long hall in a wave. By the time the screams reached the end of the hall, the entire corridor was engulfed in a cacophony of squeals and howls. It was a wave of ear-splitting, deafening sound. It wasn't nails on a chalkboard. It wasn't Jim Carrey in *Dumb and Dumber*. It was about eighty 18-year-old girls screaming in abject terror over a hall fan. The girls at the far end of the hall, I'm sure, had no idea why the wails had originated. They couldn't even hear the fan over the shrieking. It was just one girl feeding off the other. My hands covered my ears and my eyes were scrunched closed, as if the sound itself could harm my sight.

That one night was talked about for months, and I was extremely happy, at the end of my freshman year, to move on from Lewis Hall with, I felt, its faulty wiring and broken fans. Since that wild night, I had befriended a girl two doors down named Yvonne. She was vivacious, fun-loving, and had joined Delta Zeta sorority during rush. She later invited me to a Delta Zeta social where I danced and had a wonderful time with all the sisters. The next day, much to my surprise and honor, I was presented with an open bid to join Delta Zeta sorority. I immediately accepted and became a pledge sister, and Yvonne became my big sister, the person who was to guide me and be my closest friend. As such, she invited me to room with her and two other sorority sisters in the Delta Zeta apartment our sophomore year.

Lewis Hall was an old, stately, four-story building that housed the freshman women. Directly behind it was a newer, squat building, called Lewis Annex, where upper-class women lived. Lewis Annex had, at one time, housed the assistant dean of women in a small apartment. The first-floor apartment opened into the lobby and included an office, a tiny living area with a kitchen, a bedroom and bath, and a walk-in closet. In an effort to save money, the college did away with the position and opened the room for use by residents. Delta Zeta sisters made sure to occupy it each year, and it was in this room I found myself with Yvonne, Toni, and Jan. Yvonne married in December and as 1992 began, just Toni, Jan, and I occupied the apartment. As upperclassmen, Toni and Jan were no-nonsense girls who had little time for socials since it was their senior year. Toni wasn't one for grandiose stories or emotional nonsense. She was, and is, the most level-headed woman I have ever known. As a newly initiated underclassman, I was extremely honored to be asked to be a roommate with these older sisters whom I admired.

One night, late in the winter quarter as I lay in bed desperately trying to fall asleep, my mind going over and over the formulas I needed to know for my next physics exam, I could hear a piano playing. The spirit of Lewis Annex didn't have a name, but everyone knew she played the basement upright piano at random times of the day and night, and my room was positioned directly above the basement room that housed said piano. Night after night, I never heard a peep from that piano, but on this night in particular, I lay awake, eyes wide open, trying to decide what to do.

Suddenly, there was a knock at my bedroom door. It was Toni. I swiftly ran across the room and opened the door.

"What the hell?" Toni harshly whispered, "Can you hear that?"

I nodded my head.

"Well, we need to go down there and tell whoever is on that piano to knock it off! I want to sleep!" Toni bluntly stated.

If there was one thing I had learned it was that you didn't mess with Toni's love of sleep.

I wasn't a rule-breaker, and even though going to the basement in the middle of the night wasn't breaking any rules, it was against my personal rules. My parents had raised such a do-gooder and instilled such a sense of guilt in me, that I would, literally, not do any wrong because I could feel them watching over my shoulder, checking everything I did, making sure it was correct. And what was correct was going back to bed so that I could attempt to go to sleep and try to be well rested for my 8 a.m. physics class. But, Toni was a force to be reckoned with. And so, I answered, with trepidation, "Yeah! Let's go!"

As the piano continued to play a disjointed, unrecognizable tune, we whispered a plan of action to one another. We decided that Toni would go down the hall to the closest set of stairs and I would take off toward the stairs at the farthest end of the hall. We would silently descend, tip-toeing down the basement hallways until we converged in the basement common room where the piano resided. We would trap whoever, or whatever, was in there and confront it. If it was a living person, they would be soundly blessed out for keeping us awake. If it was a ghost? Well then, I'm certain we would recreate the screams from Lewis Hall the year before. The only kink in our plan was the central stairs that lead directly off the common room. Whoever, or whatever, was down there could flee up that third staircase, but they would have to go through a set of heavy doors to do it. And we would hear them.

As I lightly ran down the long hallway toward the side stairwell, my heart was pounding out of my chest. Fellow Lewis Annex residents slept behind their dorm doors, oblivious to the takedown about to happen. I quietly slipped down the stairs, making sure the heavy, metal door made not a sound as I controlled its movement. I slipped down the basement hall, still hearing the tinkling of the piano keys. I could see Toni coming toward me from the other side of the hall. Halfway to the common room, the music stopped and when we lurched into the room… there was no one there. The piano sat silent, the heavy metal doors separating the common room from the central stairs were closed, and no one had crossed in front of us to open them. We stood there, dumbfounded, incredulous, and exhausted. As we ascended the stairs and returned to our room, we tried to work out who or what could have played the piano.

"What the hell?" Toni said, exasperated. "What do you think it was?"

"I don't know," I replied. "It couldn't have been a person. There was no one there! They didn't pass us, the doors outside are locked and alarmed, and the door to the stairs would have been so loud!"

"I don't know," Toni responded. "Whoever it was could have quietly slipped up the central stairs while we came down the side stairs, and those doors can be opened quietly if you're patient."

"But still," I said, "we would have seen her through the door window as she slipped out. There's no one here!"

We slowly walked back upstairs, quietly trying to work out who, or what, could have been serenading us. We both returned to bed and didn't say a word to Jan. I never heard the piano play after that night, and I discounted most of the campus ghost stories I heard during my four years there.

Years later after our graduations when Toni and I were reminiscing about that night, she recounted something that had happened during her freshman year while living in the infamous fourth floor Lewis Hall room where the girl had purportedly hung herself. She told me how one evening when her door was open to the hallway, she was sitting on her bed doing homework. She heard someone running down the hall, toward her room, which sat at the end of the hall and directly across from the stairwell. She saw the girl in her periphery run past the door and heard her crying. And then? Silence. Toni looked up, thinking the girl was standing at her doorway, but there was no one there. She got up, looked in the corner outside her door, next to the large fan, and no one was there. The heavy metal stairway doors were closed and would have made a loud noise if opened. The hall in the other direction was empty. Toni realized, in that moment, she may have witnessed the spirit of the young student who haunted her room.

Compared to high school, my college years were fun and memorable, especially those moments that were touched by the paranormal. Those occasions only added fuel to the fire of my paranormal interests. In between my studies—and dates with Tyler—I still read any books on the paranormal I could find. The seed had been planted, and these experiences helped it sprout and grow.

UNTIL DEATH DO
TURN US TO GHOSTS

Tyler, my husband, and I met as naive, innocent teenagers while attending Space Camp in Huntsville, Alabama. It's an amazing facility where kids between the ages of 12 and 22 can "play" astronaut during a week of science, mission simulations, and teenage camaraderie. Way back in April, 1988, at the tender ages of 16, Tyler and I happened to choose the same week for our camp dates. We were placed in the same group and sat next to each other, as Payload Officers 1 and 2, during our two shuttle simulator missions. And then in Mission Control, I was Weather and Tracking, and he was the Payload Mission Officer. But, we weren't just playing astronauts. Oh, no. This was serious business, for me at least. I was determined to be West Virginia's second astronaut, and I figured I needed to get a leg up at Space Camp.

When I first met Tyler, I remember looking up. And up. And up. Even at 16, he was over six feet tall, and I had to crane my neck just to see his face. And what a cute face it was! When I looked at his eye-level name tag, I saw, "Taylor Dobson," and my first thought was "Who the heck would name their son Taylor?" Turns out that Taylor is a rather common name and I was just a sheltered hillbilly.

"Wow!" I said to the extremely tall Taylor. "Looks like we're on the same team! My name is Heather! You're Taylor?"

"Actually," he replied in a deep voice more suited to an adult man twice his age, "my name is Tyler. Nice to meet you!"

And then he smiled. And I was toast.

As we began to sit next to one another more and more during the week—me still looking up—our conversations flowed naturally. And, of course, I was smitten.

"Hey," he said. "Want a Coke?"

I hated Coke. I was, and still am, a tried and true Pepsi girl.

"Yes!" I emphatically replied, "I would love one!"

There were several girls on another team who pestered Tyler endlessly. He expressed his annoyance, and the next day as he was leaving our cafeteria table to dispose of his tray, I exclaimed, "Wait up! I'll escort you up there so those girls won't bother you!" I grabbed his forearm and stared at those harridans who dared flirt with *my* Tyler.

I'm pretty sure the crush was mutual.

We went our separate ways after that magical week in space simulation. Eventually, we began writing to one another. It wasn't until our 17th birthdays, two days apart, in February, 1989, that we called each other and our long-distance relationship began. We would speak on the phone twice a week and talk for an hour at a time, whispering sweet nothings over those long land lines. I'm sure my father loved the fact that his daughter's boyfriend lived 500 miles away. He didn't have to stay up at all hours on the weekend, waiting for me to come home from dates. His "Dad duty" consisted of peeking into my room during my twice-weekly phone calls to Tyler, pointing to his watch to let me know it was time to hang up. It was like those phone land lines tethered me to childhood much like safety lines that held the astronauts to their capsules. It was easy enough to reel me in when too much time had elapsed.

But all too soon, Tyler flew north for my junior prom and I, an only child who had never left her family for any holiday, traveled south for Thanksgiving and Christmas. With Christmas being my mother's favorite holiday, I'm sure she was brokenhearted that I left the day after Christmas for a family I hardly knew. But, back then, the strain of a long-distance relationship was a bit too much for my raging teenage hormones. Of course, time moved at a snail's pace, and the two remaining years of high school and the four years of college added up to five *hundred* teen years. I didn't want to wait for adulthood. I wanted to be with Tyler all day, every day. What I saw in Tyler, over those years, was a quiet, gentle soul who laughed at my stupid humor and thought I was beautiful. I was ready to spend the rest of my life with him.

When high school finally ended, I leapt at the chance to become a freshman at North Georgia College where Tyler would also be attending. Yes, I had an ulterior motive. My mother was disappointed that I didn't choose Case Western Reserve University in Cleveland, Ohio. I'll admit, I kept my admission there wide open and even registered for classes on the off-chance Tyler and I didn't work out, but I wanted so badly for North Georgia College to work. Though an ideal school, I already knew one person—the only person I wanted to actually be with and not just over the phone.

All through college, Tyler and I spent as much time together as classes and homework would allow. Weekends found us at his parents' house where we would eat home-cooked food and wash our clothes in a washer and dryer that didn't require quarters. College was a whirlwind of four years and soon enough, graduation loomed. As I walked across the stage, a diamond engagement ring glittered on my left hand, and eleven months later, we married in a small church in the north Georgia mountains. Poor Tyler never knew what hit him.

I never could tell Tyler about my extreme, lifelong anxiety regarding death. It wasn't something I could bring up in conversation.

"Hey, where do you want to eat, sweetie?" I would ask.

"I don't know, darlin'," he would reply. "Pizza Hut?"

"Sure!" I would say. "Hey, did you know I stay awake lots of nights freaking out about death?"

I can't even imagine the aftermath of that mic drop.

Because of my inability to talk about my fear, Tyler was plonked down into this anxiety of mine with no warning. The first time I woke him up out of a dead sleep, we were living in our small apartment in Kennesaw, Georgia. Our queen-size bed barely fit in the bedroom, and I can remember fighting back the panic that was slowly rising in my chest. I finally gave in, knowing I couldn't stop the surging terror and shook him awake, whispering his name.

When he finally awoke, confused and blinking, he asked, concerned, "What's wrong?"

"I can't sleep!" I breathlessly replied. "I'm thinking about death and infinity!"

At this point in my early years of life, my parents would begin their sorrowful attempt at calming me down. Now, Tyler just looked at me, wrapped his arms around me, and said, "It's okay. I've got you." He promptly turned on the television and let me watch until we both fell asleep.

Luckily for Tyler, those late-night wake-ups were few and far between because in my short 20-odd years, I had learned many coping mechanisms for shutting down my restless brain. Once our children were born, though, all bets were off. My hormones and body chemistry had been upended by childbirth, and I couldn't control any of it on my own. Our twins, Amelia and Heath, were six weeks premature and spent three weeks in the Neonatal ICU. Although their health problems were extremely mild in nature—they simply needed to gain weight and strength to take in eight bottles a day—I would still wake up at all hours of the night, worried that I would arrive at the NICU the next day to find one or both of them had died. I worried the nurse would drop them or they would pass from Sudden Infant Death Syndrome. My obstetrician tried prescribing me sleep aids, medication that would knock me out for eight hours. Unfortunately, my anxiety was such that I would take the medication and still wake up two hours later. I was somehow existing on two hours of sleep each night. Later, when Amelia and Heath came home from the hospital, those late-night feedings were coupled with panic attacks, and it was only with the addition of anti-depressant medication that it lessened. Unfortunately, I repeated the same pattern with our third child, Jarrod.

One night, six months after the birth of Jarrod, my dear friend Teri coaxed me out of the house with the promise of two tickets to a local ghost tour and dinner. We spent two hours in the dark, November chill, listening to the tragic and scary stories of Civil War ghosts and other paranormal shenanigans in suburban Atlanta, Georgia. We didn't see any spirits but nonetheless enjoyed ourselves. After the tour, a local author who had written a book about local hauntings, was signing copies of her books, and I asked her if she knew of any groups in the area who conducted paranormal investigations. She pointed me in the direction of one in particular, and I thanked her. As I walked away, I clutched my newest ghost book to my chest, determined to read it during late-night bottle feedings with my six-month-old son. Teri and I decamped to a local diner and excitedly talked about the tour while wolfing down a late dinner. We both thought investigating ghosts would be an amazing experience and couldn't believe my luck in finding a group in the Atlanta area.

Upon arriving home, I regaled Tyler with stories from the tour. Excitement colored my voice as I told him I could join a local group that investigated haunted homes and businesses, just like the people on the *Ghost Hunters* TV show. He nodded his head, blinked a few times, and said only these words:

"Just don't bring anything home with you."

The next morning, with great trepidation, I logged onto the message board of the group I had been told of and introduced myself. I told the members how excited I was to be a part of something so incredible and then promptly deflated when I realized the majority of the investigations and meetings were on the other side of Atlanta, over an hour from my home. There was no way I could drive great distances while still being mom to a six-month-old baby. I was crushed. I stewed over it for a couple of weeks and finally found the nerve to email the author I had met. I asked her if she knew of any paranormal investigative groups closer to my home in Woodstock. She quickly replied that she was starting a group in the area, and I was welcome to join. The first meeting would be in one month, in January, 2008.

I was ecstatic, and I pitched the idea to Tyler.

"Hey, hon?" I tentatively asked a few weeks after the tour. "I want to join a ghost hunting team."

Tyler just looked at me, wide-eyed.

I quickly reminded him, "You know, like the TV show? *Ghost Hunters*? Except it's a team just a few miles from here, and I would be going to people's houses, looking for evidence of ghosts."

"Um," he replied, "when would you do this?"

"Oh! That's the best part," I gushed. "It would be at night on the weekends! Jarrod is finally sleeping through the night and no longer needs midnight bottles, so I wouldn't miss out on anything!"

"Are you sure you want to do something like this?" he asked. "What about your fear of death?"

"Well," I calmly put forth. "These latest panic attacks have nothing to do with me and everything to do with Amelia, Heath, and Jarrod. I want concrete answers for them and not suppositions. Someday, they're going to realize they will die and will want to know what's going to happen. I need to be able to answer them and know that what I'm telling them is the truth."

He looked at me, took a deep breath, and, as before, responded, "Just don't bring anything home with you."

From my first investigation to my most recent, before I leave for the evening, Tyler asks where I'm going and who is going with me. He tells me to have a good time, be safe, kisses me goodbye, and repeats those same seven words. When I return late in the night, the hall light has been left on, and the bed sheets turned down. As I slide onto my pillow, Tyler will pat my leg and fall back asleep. The next morning, he'll ask me how it went and listen intently as I recount the events.

Through the many years, Tyler has been there, front row and center at DragonCon panels, library presentations, paranormal team Christmas parties, and late-night critique sessions of *Ghost Adventures*. I continue to investigate, to question, and to explore all the possibilities of what the paranormal could be. Tyler quietly supports me through my paranormal journey in different ways. He gifts me with paranormal equipment when our budget allows and even considers my fellow paranormal investigators as his friends. He willingly watches the paranormal reality shows I dutifully record and pick apart, even chiming in with his own opinion on their antics.

In 2011, my sweet, quiet husband found himself spending eight hours wandering the cavernous hallways of Waverly Hills Sanatorium. He didn't say much during that night, but his tall, imposing shadow followed me wherever I went. He quietly listened and watched, standing guard over me while small, ghostly shadows flitted in the periphery. When a flashlight turned on seemingly by itself, unseen hands controlling the on/off button, answering yes/no questions from our investigators, he gasped in surprise. His eyes were wide as he took it all in, and at the end of the night, he said to me, "I get it. I understand why you do this. It's the quest to answer the unknown."

He's never asked since to repeat the experience.

Through it all, he's only ever had one request: "Just don't bring anything home with you."

And I do my best to oblige the love of my life.

ATHEISM AND
THE PARANORMAL

I am a daughter, wife, mother, writer, paranormal investigator, and atheist.

Each of those labels are quirks of biology, marital law, procreation, career, and passion. That last one, though, is the most contentious of all the labels I have ever, and will ever, hold. Few labels can bring out the ire and rush to judgment that "atheist" can. It's very confusing to me because it's a label I'm very proud of, yet one that I have to keep close to my chest. Living in the Bible Belt means that your worth is closely tied to where you go to church and what you believe. Proclaiming disbelief will almost always end in a shunning from the community, and that's something my children and I have had to learn firsthand. I've had family members turn their backs on me because of my atheism, and my youngest had friends reject him because he admitted that he may not believe in God. Honesty is not always the best policy when people ask us about our beliefs.

My "religion" label, if you will, was originally thanks to the geography of my upbringing. I was raised in the Presbyterian church, which makes sense considering the large number of Scotch-Irish immigrants who settled in West Virginia in the 18th century and brought the

Presbyterian church—an offshoot of the Church of Scotland—with them. If I had been born in Minnesota, I'd most likely be Lutheran, or if I were a product of Alabama, I'd most likely be Baptist. My journey to atheism wasn't a spontaneous one. It happened after many years of earnest faithfulness, quiet reflection, research, and calling myself anything but atheist before I would finally admit, at the age of 42, that I was, truly, an atheist.

I now realize that my journey to atheism began in childhood, when I felt there were many inconsistencies between Christian beliefs and what I observed in the world around me. I struggled to be a good Christian, following the Ten Commandments and trying to love everyone, even if they were hard to love. Yet, when I would attend the funeral of a fellow church member, knowing they had violated many of those commandments or the basic tenet of love, they would still be declared a citizen of Heaven.

I distinctly remember my Sunday School teacher telling me that one uttered curse word would send me to Hell, and when I accidentally let one fly several months later, in the midst of a bloody bicycle accident, I was convinced the gates to Heaven would be immediately padlocked upon my death. I was terrified that I would now have to spend an eternity burning in Hellfire with the likes of murderers and rapists… for one cuss word.

I've always had an analytical mind, and I feel that in order to believe something, I need to experience that something with all of my senses. I can remember watching the crowd around me at my first high school boyfriend's church. During the hymns and sermons, people would raise their hands toward the sky and begin shouting, "Amen!" or "Hallelujah!" and I could see that they were affected by the words being spoken or sung, and I felt… nothing. There was no quiver of excitement or surge of exquisite happiness. There was only me, feeling confused, sad, and excluded. I would watch those moments with widened eyes and speculated as to what was wrong with me.

Oh, well, maybe it's because I'm a kid. That's mostly adults doing that. Maybe when I finally grow up, I'll have those ecstatic emotions.

But… it never happened. Not when I attended a charismatic church in my 20s or my in-laws' Baptist church in my 30s. No matter how many denominations I tried, how many church services I attended, I never felt that all-encompassing presence of God that others felt.

As I matured, I understood that I wasn't at fault, that I wasn't deliberately trying to avoid these snippets of higher understanding. I came to comprehend that I was wired differently from others and that I would probably never have those experiences. When I realized this, it was like being hit by a truck. The shock and fear were all-encompassing and the pain of not having anything to believe in, of knowing there was nothing watching over me, was overwhelming. I wanted to believe, I wanted to have something there to hold on to because that would be comforting and normal. I began to ask myself why would God deliberately create a person who could never experience Him? It was when I applied Occam's razor—a problem-solving principle that states the simpler explanation is the only explanation—that I concluded there is no God and I'm not faulty or incorrect. I just *am*. And to never have a religious experience is the norm and not the exception. Many of those other people may not be having those experiences and may be acting for the crowd because they need acceptance.

When I announced to family, friends, and acquaintances that I was now a paranormal investigator, it resulted in a combination of either strange looks, head shakes and subject changes, widened eyes, exclamations, or questions involving when said party could join me on my next investigation. For the most part, though, there was a sort of wonderment, whether positive or negative, and many questions. For me, if the person also knows I'm an atheist and a paranormal investigator, the biggest question they have is, "How can you reconcile your atheism with the idea of an afterlife?" No matter how many times this question is posed of me, I'm always surprised by it, that the only way one can believe in an afterlife is if one also has faith in a higher power. For me, the two are mutually exclusive of one another.

When I joined my first paranormal investigative group, I was surprised to discover that I wasn't the only atheist who investigated the paranormal. As we all settled in to our roles and became more comfortable with each other, we inevitably began talking about our lives, and this included our beliefs. Sitting around the table at J. Christopher's or lounging on the couches at the local coffee shop, our monthly meetings evolved from just old and new business to finding out more about one another. As we hugged our coffee mugs, these huddles helped us to get to know one another. We found out that we were a healthy mix of Christians, Pagans, New Age Spiritualists, and even a couple of atheists, all driven by one common goal: we wanted to know the definitive answer of what happens to us after we die. We eventually became more than just a team that worked well together; we became a family.

I think it's because of my atheism, coupled with my analytical mind, that I'm able to walk into a home and attempt to answer the question, "What is causing this activity?" with the answer, "It's explainable and normal."

So many paranormal investigators immediately jump to the "paranormal conclusion" which, ironically, hurts the paranormal community. I recall one investigation in Canton, Georgia, where the homeowners had called in a local paranormal group to investigate their activity, only to be told that whatever was happening was evil. The clients were ready to move out of their house, but lucky for them, they called us for a second opinion. What was classified as demonic by one group, was actually a family of squirrels living in their attic and the completely natural night terrors suffered by their four-year-old daughter. By looking first for the rational answers and applying Occam's razor, we were able to give them a rational explanation for what was happening. A quick peak into the attic confirmed the existence of squirrels, particularly when we saw their glowing eyes and found their nest amongst the insulation. My own three-year-old was experiencing night terrors during this time, and I was able to see the exact same behavior in their daughter that I witnessed many times with my son.

Whenever we investigate, our goal is to find the rational, or natural, explanation and only if we can't find one do we then move on to paranormal explanations. Do the cabinet doors open because they're not level? Are the noises in the attic attributable to wildlife? Are the disembodied voices actually the neighbors talking outside with their voices being projected? I want to make absolutely sure that whatever is happening can be easily explained before I jump to the paranormal conclusion. Then, only when I can't rationally explain what is happening, do I reach for the paranormal. By doing this, I am helping secure the study of the paranormal to someday be considered a valid scientific field of study and not a hobby of ridicule.

Investigating in the Bible Belt presents its own unique set of problems. Many Southern Baptists believe that when a person dies, they either pass on to Heaven or to Hell, that there is no in between and any actual paranormal activity must be inhuman, or evil, in nature. So many of our phone calls and emails are from clients who are panicked. Take, for example, the couple in Senoia who thought the shadow figure in their teenage son's bedroom was something malevolent. Or the veteran in Toccoa who was convinced that the spirit in his home was inhuman. Neither of these cases were evil in nature, as both turned out to be rather benign. Being able to walk into a client's home and having the neutrality of atheism and science gives me the ability to step back and observe without any preconceived notions of religion or belief. Also, having many years of quiet, uneventful investigations under my belt has allowed me to look at these clients and say, with confidence, "There is nothing evil here. I've never seen anything evil. There is nothing to fear." Now, that doesn't mean that inhuman spirits don't exist, but my lack of experience with anything of that nature helps to reinforce the rarity of such occurrences.

The most important part of investigating as an atheist is that I don't announce my beliefs—or lack thereof—to the clients. As I've stated, I'm a paranormal investigator in the South, and the Christian belief in God and Jesus Christ is more pervasive here than Chick-fil-A restaurants and football. As a paranormal investigator, my priority is helping the client, no matter their faith or beliefs, even if they clash with mine, which they almost always do.

Whenever I walk into a crowd of people, maybe at a middle school band performance or a PTA meeting, the crosses worn around the necks of numerous believers—gold, silver, small, large, with or without gemstones—twinkle and sparkle like a mirror ball at a discotheque. They reflect the tastes of the wearer and are quite beautiful and quite ubiquitous here in Woodstock, Georgia. After years of living as an atheist, I wondered if I should find something I could wear, something small and unobtrusive, that would subtly announce to the world my lack of belief. As I searched the Internet for "atheist jewelry," I was disappointed with the limited choices, all of them a large "A" surrounded by a circle and most of them too big and too flashy for my tastes. I took this as a reminder that even though I provide information about my atheism when asked, I don't walk around pronouncing it to the world at large. So, I admire the ability of the local faithful to announce their religion around their neck and keep my disbelief a private matter.

BEING A MOM AND
A GHOST HUNTER

Motherhood was not a foregone conclusion for me. Intellectually, I knew I would probably be a mother. Simply because of my heterosexuality and the presence of my female reproductive organs, I assumed that I would most likely have children in the future. But, it wasn't something I obsessed over. I didn't play with dolls and I didn't fantasize about pregnancy. All I knew was that I wanted to get married and wait a few years before the inevitable procreation happened because I had too many friends who were the products of divorce and broken homes, and I didn't want that to happen to my children.

But then, when the day finally happened that I threw away my birth control pills and made a conscious decision to have children... I found out I couldn't. My reproductive system, due to a simple quirk of biology, was misfiring. I was living with a body that produced far too much of one hormone and not enough of the others, and that meant I was infertile. When I discovered this, I became haunted by my inadequacy. I mean, seriously? I was standing there, with double-X chromosomes, a uterus ready to go, and no way to make any of it work without the miracle of modern medicine.

Eventually, after many tears, heartaches, thousands of dollars, and four years, the unexpected happened. I discovered I was pregnant and not just pregnant, but *pregnant*. With twins Amelia and Heath! Really! After all of that struggle, being a mom was suddenly a reality!

Before I even began to show, I was at the Motherhood Maternity store, buying maternity pants and shirts. I was so excited and immediately started picking out paint colors for the nursery and registering for cribs and a stroller. Stores like Babies R Us were happy to help me register for all the baby things I may or may not need. There were diapers and formula—times two—and little pink and blue clothes and soft, pastel blankets and… wow. It was nuts, and I had no idea.

Six weeks before their due date, my labor was induced due to pre-eclampsia. Within a few hours, Tyler and I went from a family of two to a family of four. Amelia and Heath spent their first 20 days of life in the NICU, gaining weight and learning the suck-swallow-breathe reflex. I was an emotional wreck, being suddenly dropped into the deep end of life with both arms full of tiny preemie babies. I didn't really have much time to think or process everything through. When they finally came home, the sleepless nights, endless diapers, and boundless joy began!

And then? We went and did it again without all the doctors or shots or embarrassing exams. Four days after the twins' first birthday, I found out I was pregnant a second time. This time, thankfully, it was just one baby, and nine months later we found ourselves the parents of another little boy. Slowly, but surely, as I adapted to being a mom of twins, I figured out how to be a mom to three kids under the age of two. It was an absolute whirlwind ride. Eventually, they all grew out of babyhood and graduated from pacifiers to door knob covers, toys, and more toys. Now, though, thirteen years later, the toys are giving way to computers, video games, and hover boards. The latest "toys" are more expensive, and I find myself driving to Goodwill, hoping the My Little Pony and Lego sets will find good homes. Amelia, Heath, and Jarrod have added so much joy to our family, and I never before knew that being a mother could be such an amazing and fulfilling experience.

As I've grown into motherhood, I've thoroughly enjoyed watching them mature and figure out what it means to be human. I've learned that the hardest part isn't what most moms experience:

Transitioning to solid food? So easy.

Potty training? That was nothing.

Realizing they would someday die? That was the worst.

It all started when we took in my mother's cat, Bandit. I had bought Bandit for her after Dad died, while she still lived in West Virginia. She was lonely, and I wanted to fix that. After she moved to Georgia, Bandit came with her, but eventually she realized her allergies were making life with him miserable. Bandit was a good cat but absolutely adored my mother. Here, at our home, I could tell he was heartbroken as he tended to stay away from the family, preferring to remain hidden from the kids who were precocious and into everything. One day, six months after Bandit moved in, my mother came over for a visit. She found Bandit on the stairs, and after petting him, she came to me, holding him, panicked that something was terribly wrong. And she was right. We rushed him to the vet, hope in our eyes, only to be told that he was in advanced kidney failure and that our only option was to painlessly hasten his end. My mother and I sobbed as Bandit took his last breaths and then quickly realized that the hardest was yet to come.

"Hey, kids, come here," I gently called to Amelia, Heath, and Jarrod, waving them into the family room. "Mama needs to talk to you."

They put down their toys and padded in to where I sat on the floor. The twins were cognizant five-year-olds and Jarrod was a precocious three. I made sure I was positioned at their eye level, not towering above them as an authority figure but small so that they could see my sincerity.

"I have something very sad to tell you," I began.

"Oh, Mama," Amelia replied, concern in her sweet, young eyes. "What is it?"

"Bandit was very sick, and so Nana and I had to take him to the doctor today."

"What's wrong wif him?" Heath lisped.

"Part of his body stopped working, a really important part. And because of that, he died." I told them, tears already squeezing out of my eyes.

All three of them looked at me, confused. "What do you mean he died, Mama? What does that mean?" Jarrod asked.

I took a deep breath, "Well, honey, it means that his body stopped working. He will never come back to us. It's like he went to sleep, but he won't ever wake up."

There was a pause and then the tears began flowing. It was absolutely heartrending listening to them cry. The questions flew, and I spent the next hour answering everything from "Mama? Is Bandit with PawPaw Tom now?" to "Can we see him?" Gradually, their tears subsided and they became bored, moving off to play with each other. The resiliency of children is amazing, but I knew that this was simply the calm before the storm. There was more yet to come.

Two years later, Amelia asked me, "Mama, do you remember Bandit?"

"Yes, sweetie, of course I do," I replied. "What about him?"

"Well, he died." she said, rather matter-of-factly, "And Paw-Paw Tom, he died, too, right?"

"Yes," I said, terrified of where this was going to go.

"Am I going to die?"

And there it was. The bombshell. The day I had been dreading had arrived.

"Yes. Everyone eventually dies. Bandit, Paw-Paw Tom, Nana, me, Papa, and you."

She took a moment, her eyes widened, and the panic set it.

"But I don't want to die! I don't wanna die, Mama! *Don't let me die!*"

All I could do was hold her, kiss her head, and rock her, whispering words of comfort. It was, absolutely, without a doubt, one of the worst moments of my life. There were many sleepless nights after that when her mind would race and inevitably go to scary places. We would snuggle in the bed, watch TV, and I would answer every question she put to me as honestly as I could.

"Mama. What happens to us after we die?" she asked in a very small voice.

"I don't know, sweetie. I don't know what exactly is going to happen," I responded. "But I absolutely, positively know that we all continue to exist, and that there's nothing to fear."

Eventually, she calmed, but for Tyler and I, that calm wouldn't last for very long because Heath's moment came just a few months later and Jarrod followed closely behind his older brother. While Jarrod responded much like Amelia, with many questions and tears, Heath was quieter. He would slip into our bed late at night, unannounced. I would ask, "What's wrong?" and he would respond with one word:

"Death."

He spoke volumes with that one word. But, he would listen to what I said to Amelia, and for him, that was enough.

Before and even after we mostly conquered their fears about death, my children still feared the dark and the monsters they were convinced existed in their closets, under their beds, and in the dim corners of their rooms. The monsters, it seems, had gone from existing only in their minds to inhabiting our physical world. My first encounter with their childhood monsters happened, of course, on a dark night. We had put the kids in bed, dealt with the endless requests for more hugs and sips of water. Finally, the lights were turned off, and Tyler and I gratefully sighed and collapsed into our bed. Soon enough, though, I heard Amelia's door open.

"Mama?"

"What is it, Miss-Miss?" I wearily asked.

"There's a monster under my bed."

Externally, I just looked at her. Internally, though, I screamed, ripped out my hair, and cried huge tears of exhaustion.

"Honey, there's nothing under your bed." I said, "I pinky-swear promise that your room is monster-free."

"But Mama… It's *there!* I *know* it is!"

"Okay! Okay!" I said, exasperated. "Just get into our bed and sleep with us."

And so, she gleefully wiggled onto our bed, planted herself in between us, and snuggled under the covers. Tyler and I looked at each other, faces sagging with fatigue. We turned out the lights and an hour later, she fell asleep in our bed, feet pressed into my kidneys, happily snoring away. While she slept, I fumed. When I was sure she wouldn't wake up, I carried her into her bed, thankful that young children could sleep through both hurricanes and clumsy mothers.

Much like the movie *Groundhog Day*, this scene repeated itself for many, many… many nights. As I started to look like Bill Murray from the lack of sleep, I became more and more resigned to the fact that this was now my life. Every night, she would express her abject fear, I would try to convince her otherwise, and she would still demand a thorough check of every nook and cranny. I would huff and roll my eyes, getting down on the floor to make a show of looking underneath her bed. I would stay for at least a minute, moving up and down the length of the bed, swiping my arm underneath to show her it wasn't being eaten. Rather, I would end up pulling out dust bunnies, paper, a pair of slippers, a stuffed animal, a doll… basically everything in the free world. Heath and Jarrod would silently watch from the doorway, absorbing the whole process. I would clean away the detritus, showing her every single thing I had found and putting it all away. Then, I looked inside her closet. I made a big show of moving aside her clothes and shoes, showing her that there was nothing inside. And then, I went the extra mile and securely closed and blocked the door. Still, she would insist there was a monster. So, I got down again and took a picture of the underside of her bed with my phone.

I showed her the picture and her response was, "The monster is 'invidible,' Mama!"

Whatever it was she conjured out of her imagination, she was convinced that it was there, and no amount of parental comfort convinced her otherwise. Either that or she had figured out how to play me like a Stradivarius. If she wasn't in our bed, bruising our organs with her flailing feet, then I was crammed into her bed, waiting for her to fall asleep, getting punched in the head, wondering how long it would be before she outgrew this fear and I could get a full night's sleep. I remembered lying there, convinced that I would still be doing this in her college years.

"Moooo-ooom! Could you drive up to campus tonight?" she would wail over the phone.

"Why? It's 100 miles up there!" I would say, perturbed. "It will be close to midnight before I get there!"

"Well, I've got a math test tomorrow that you can help me study for, and I also need you to check my dorm room for monsters."

And away I would drive to the State University of You've Spent Way Too Much Money On This Tuition so that I can check under the bed of my 19-year-old daughter who is currently signed up to get a major in journalism, but she's thinking about changing it to early childhood education and adding two years to her schedule because she waits until her senior year to make up her mind.

Finally, after cooking up all the different scenarios in my mind, my sleep-addled brain had a brilliant idea. After that late night and too-early morning, I found myself putting away my paranormal investigative equipment from a weekend investigation. As I bagged up my Thermos, flashlight, and digital audio recorder, I came across the newest "member" of my equipment bag: my K2 meter. A K2 meter is just a fancy electromagnetic (EM) field detector. It's a piece of equipment that electricians use to detect faulty wiring but, because of the hypothesis that ghosts and spirits emit high EM fields when they manifest, paranormal investigators now use them as well. The great thing about a K2 meter is that it has lights, and as the EM field around it increases in strength, the lights change from green to yellow to red. And I knew that this was something I could use in the fight against the "invidible" monsters of Amelia's room.

That night, as I wished Amelia good dreams, she firmly declared, yet again, that she wouldn't go to sleep because of the ever-present monsters, and that's when I pulled the greatest hat-trick of my motherhood career out of my pajama pocket.

"Miss-Miss!" I exclaimed, "Look at this! It's my K2 meter!"

"What is it, Mama?" she whispered in wonder, reaching for it.

"You know how I sometimes go to people's houses on the weekend to go looking for ghosts and monsters?" I asked.

"Uh-huh!" she nodded her head. "You're a ghost hunter!"

"Well, this is a K2 meter, and it has really pretty lights. Do you see the lights?!" And I pushed the side button to make the lights change from green, to yellow, to red.

"Oooo! Pretty!" she exhaled.

"The lights only go off if there's a ghost or a monster nearby." I said. "So, why don't we take this K2 meter and put it under your bed? And if it goes off, we'll know the invisible monster is there."

"Okay, Mama. I'll help."

We got down on the floor together and moved the K2 meter the length of her bed. And, of course, the meter cooperated and stayed green. Then, we repeated the process in her closet. As I moved the meter under and behind her clothes, I heard a noise at the door. Heath and Jarrod had arrived and were eager to help.

"Mama!" Heath exclaimed, "Can I see? Can I do it?"

And so it was that I found my three little future ghost hunters doing an EMF sweep with a K2 meter. They each took turns holding the meter, moving it around the closet and then back under the bed for good measure. The boys were fascinated, and Amelia, of course, directed them since it was her room. Once they were satisfied that Amelia's room was monster-free, they all tottered into the boys' room, using the K2 meter to check under their beds and inside their closet. Amazingly enough, Amelia was satisfied with the results, and the boys thought I was the coolest mom ever. We all said our goodnights and everyone fell asleep soon thereafter.

The next night, Amelia again claimed the monster was there, but I told her that was impossible because I had visited her room while she was at preschool and chased it away, which, of course, meant I had a mug of coffee and did absolutely nothing, but sometimes white lies are a parent's best defense.

"Mama," she ordered, "I want to check it. It's my room."

Of course, I couldn't refuse her, so I hauled the meter out of my equipment bag and patiently watched from the doorway as she expertly ran the K2 around inside her closet and underneath her bed. When the meter unfailingly stayed green, she was satisfied that the invisible monster of her nightmares was gone for good.

"I think we must have scared it away, Mama," she said, very seriously.

"I think so, too, honey," I emphatically agreed.

"Those lights must be too bright," she pondered, "and since those invidible monsters only like dark, they run away from the lights."

"Exactly, Miss-Miss!" I said, "And you know what? Ghost hunters sometimes hunt monsters, too, and I promise that if I ever find a monster in your room, I'll call in Mister Jordan and Mister Clint and Miss Stefanie, and we'll get rid of it for you. Okay?"

"Okay, Mama!"

Never again was our home plagued by childhood nightmares living in the dark places. Only clothes occupied the closet and only cobwebs lived in the basement. The floor under their beds remained empty— except for the crap that got pushed back under there—and stayed monster-free. And I firmly believe that my K2 meter is the reason why our nights have remained terror-free in the many years since.

Since those nights, I have shared this story with friends and family and told them to put away their baby gift registries, sell off their cloth diapers, and instead invest in a bag full of paranormal equipment. It could be the best investment they ever make. I should probably contact the CEO of Amazon and tell him that K2 meters should be included in baby registries.

As each child has come to me with the realization of their death, I am ready and able to tell them that death won't be an ending, but rather a transition. I am excited to teach them that life takes on many forms and that death isn't an end to everything, but a passage from one existence to another. In the intervening years, I have shown them a video of a door opening by itself, of an EMF meter moving on its own, and played audio files of disembodied voices speaking to us. I watch as their eyes open wide with wonder. I have proof that death is absolutely nothing to fear and that, until then, we can live and grow and experience everything this amazing life has to offer to take with us to the next life.

As time has gone by, we've lost family, friends, and pets to the inescapable entropy. Each time I've had to tell my children that someone we've loved is now gone, the telling has never been easy. The tears have never lessened, and the grief of loss remains. But the fear isn't there. My children don't panic over the idea of death the way I did as a child. The late-night anxiety doesn't exist. I had no idea when I started this journey that it would be so fulfilling for not just me, but also for my family. Yes, friendships and connections have been made. But the peace my work has brought to my children, and myself, has been the most rewarding part. It's a peace I wouldn't give up for the world.

QUANTUM FLUX

I was the drum major for my junior high and high school marching bands. I loved the idea of being out front, leading my fellow musicians, and let's face it... I was a bit bossy. During football and band festival marching seasons, I had a large, wooden podium from which I conducted. Someone had to move that awkward block of wood across the field at the exact moment I would need it, and that someone was my Dad. He would borrow a neighbor's pickup truck, drive the podium to whatever far-off high school football field we were performing at that particular Saturday. And then, rain or shine, as the South Charleston High School Black Eagles Marching Band marched across the field, taking center stage for our 10-minute performance, he would race across the sideline, pushing the podium on a dolly, precisely placing it just as my foot hit the bottom step.

Dad and Mom were like this for every performance. Whether it was a Girl Scouts play in fourth grade or a soggy, cold homecoming game, they were there. It was obvious that I was a daddy's girl. It didn't help matters that I was an only child and that my parents could dote on me as much as they wanted without fear of favoritism. It used to steam me when people would ask my birth order within my family and, upon finding out my status as an only child, would immediately respond with a snotty, "Oh! You must be spoiled rotten!" Well, of course I got all the Christmas gifts, and of course I got all the attention, but I still received my fair share of punishment if I screwed up, and having all the attention isn't a good thing when you're a young adult trying to sprout your wings and fly. My father and I had similar interests. We enjoyed science fiction and had the same corny sense of humor. It didn't take much for us to laugh, and for many years, he was my best friend.

When my father died on January 30th, 1998, it was sudden and unexpected, but not wholly surprising. He was unhealthy for most of his later years and even though, deep down, my mother and I knew he wouldn't live to a ripe old age, we didn't expect his 66th birthday to be his last. He had checked into the VA hospital the day before, all set for a heart catheterization, a regular procedure that thousands of Americans have performed on them every year. He called me at my home in Cumming, shortly before he drove the thirty minutes to the hospital, expressing his fears over the day ahead.

"Heather, I don't think I'm going to come out of this one," he said, worry coloring his voice.

"Oh, Dad," I brushed him off. "If you had died all the times you said you were going to die, I'd have a grave dug to China by now."

We continued talking, turning to lighter subjects such as my upcoming 26th birthday and the weather. When he hung up, I shook my head, already thinking about my day and all the things I had to do at work. I've regretted that conversation and my harsh words in the years since.

When my mother called the next day, I expected to hear the usual humdrum, "Oh, he's fine. We'll be home tomorrow" update. Instead, I received the unexpected.

"Heather, your father had a heart attack during the procedure," she told me.

"Should I come home?" I worriedly asked.

"No," she responded, "everything should be all right. They've given him blood thinners and are going to let him rest tonight, and then tomorrow, he'll have an angioplasty done."

And I hung up the phone, confident that he would be just fine because my mother said everything would be copasetic.

The next morning dawned, and my mother frantically called me.

"Heather, you need to get up here," she practically shouted into the phone. "Your father has a brain tumor, and the blood thinners caused it to start bleeding last night. One whole side of his body is paralyzed, and his body temperature is dropping."

I was stunned. I didn't know what to say and just sat there, mouth open, unresponsive.

Over the years, Dad's personality had changed. It wasn't very noticeable at first, and now that I look back, I realize that the warning signs were all there. He became very unsure of every decision placed before him and would cry at the drop of a hat. When I would make my twice-weekly phone calls, half the time Dad wouldn't talk to me, choosing instead to whisper questions and responses in my mother's ear so that she could communicate with me. Rather than respond to this worrisome behavior with concern for his health, I became frustrated and chose instead to shut him out, annoyed that I was suddenly the adult in our relationship and he was the child. Before my very eyes, my sweet, happy father turned into a confused, sad mess, and I responded not with compassion and love but with fear and frustration. That unknown brain tumor, though, wasn't finished with my father, and it wasn't the heart attack that would end him, but this small growth in his brain.

"They're going to transfer him to St. Mary's Medical Center across town, perform a CT scan, and then do surgery to remove the tumor or to stop it from bleeding any further, and then they'll do the angioplasty," Mom continued, "but you should probably come home."

As soon as I hung up the phone, I called Tyler, and we set in motion the day to come. Friends from work descended on our home and helped me pack. Tyler booked two plane tickets and rented a car, and within hours, we were in Charleston, West Virginia, driving over the speed limit toward St. Mary's in Huntington. It was 6:30 p.m. when Tyler pulled into the parking lot, and before he set the parking brake, I was out of the car, speed walking to the front entrance. By the time I made it to the front information desk, Tyler had caught up to me.

"Excuse me," I nervously said to the nurse. "My name is Heather Dobson, and my father, Thomas Scarbro, is a patient here. Could you tell me his room number?"

She began scrolling through her patient list, found my father's name, and paused.

"Oh, yes, Mrs. Dobson," she tentatively replied, "I'll need you to come down the hall with me."

She led us just a few doors down a hall off the main entrance. As we neared the doorway, I could see Sarah and Vicky, two of my mother's friends. Tyler and I walked into the room and standing off to the side were my mother and a nun. I was confused.

"Heather," my mother said, "he's gone. Your father died on the operating table."

And that was it for me. I don't think the noise I made was human. It was a noise of pain, sadness, regret, anger, and loneliness, all rolled into one. Immediately, I was surrounded. Sarah, Vicky, Mom, Tyler, and the nun were all there, whispering words of calm and comfort, touching me, trying to give me peace, but none of it was working. All I wanted was my father, and they couldn't give him to me. After a few minutes, a nurse came in and quietly told us that they had cleaned up my father's body, and we could go in to the operating room and view him.

As we walked in to the OR, it was surreal. There my father lay, covered in a sheet with his head and shoulders exposed. There was a little bit of dried blood around his nostrils that the nurses had missed. He was as white as the sheet covering him and his chest remained still, his lungs no longer expanding and contracting with breath, his heart no longer beating. I stared, willing him to do something, hoping he would open his eyes, look at me, and say my name. I started to cry because I knew in that moment that I would never again hear his voice. The nun asked if she could say a prayer, and I nodded my head, knowing my father would have appreciated that. As the others bowed their heads, I refused to follow suit. Eyes open, standing at his bedside, I watched his still form, listening to the nun praying beside us. I looked for any sign that he had fooled the doctors and was still alive. But despite my vigilance, he remained absolutely still.

He was truly gone.

After the prayer, we filed out of the room. I didn't want to leave, but I knew it was pointless to stay. And so I turned my back on my partner-in-crime and walked out of the hospital, facing life as a fatherless adult.

Mom and I obeyed his final wishes and had him cremated. A week later, I returned to Georgia and my job, crushed and sadder than I had ever been in my entire life. My mother was left behind in West Virginia to adjust to her life without her husband. I was brokenhearted. For fourteen days, I slowly discovered my new normal, until Mom called me to tell me that she had found my father's older brother, my Uncle Curtis, dead in his apartment. I couldn't believe it. The two most important men in my life besides Tyler were gone. My Uncle Curtis had helped raise me alongside my parents, and during the week of my father's visitations and funerals, I could tell he was utterly devastated. In my 26 years, I had never seen him cry. I think he cried enough tears after my father's death to make up for a lifetime of a stoic stiff-upper-lip. The medical examiner determined that he died of a heart attack, and it wasn't until three days after his death that my mother checked up on him and found him face-down in his one-bedroom apartment. His death haunts her to this day, and that visual of finding him greeted her many months thereafter whenever she would close her eyes. Even though his death certificate said "heart attack," Mom and I knew he really died of a broken heart. He adored my father, his younger brother, and couldn't live without him.

Again, I found myself on a plane to West Virginia. As I was the executrix of Uncle Curtis's estate—$6,000 and more photography equipment than you could shake a stick at—it was up to me to take care of his final wishes and have him cremated as well. I was so very sick and tired of funeral homes, death certificates, and deciding who got what keepsake that I didn't even bat an eye when Mom said she would keep both sets of ashes behind her bedroom door until we decided what to do with them. It would be three months before I could make it back to West Virginia to bury their ashes in the spring.

Not long after my father died, my mother called me, breathless, one morning.

"Heather. The strangest thing happens every night," she said. "I can hear your father in this house."

"What?!" I replied, incredulous, "You're joking."

"No!" she said, emphatically, "I can hear the floorboards creak and groan. I'll hear the bathroom door open and close, the toilet flushes, and then I hear him walking into the kitchen. A few minutes later, I'll hear the floorboards creak again as he walks through the living room, down the hall, and into the bedroom. I just lay there, wide awake, waiting for a knock on the door or something. It's creepy!"

My father was a proponent of midnight snacking and, as such, during his life, would take a nightly trip out of his bedroom, to the bathroom—where, of course, he would take care of important business and flush—walk down the hall, through the living room, and into the kitchen, where he would rustle up something sweet to eat. When finished, he would travel back to his bedroom and resume his rest.

As I would later learn, what my mother was experiencing was a residual haunting. This wasn't muscle memory, her ears "hearing" these noises because they were expected. Neither was this an intelligent spirit that was roaming the house and could interact with her. This was most likely an imprint, akin to a tape recording, playing over and over again, due to repeated actions or because of one highly emotional or violent act. Somehow, moments like my father's wanderings are imprinted on a location, and the living can be witness to them. There is no "play" button or anything that "activates" the ghostly recording. It just happens.

My father's nightly visits to the bathroom and kitchen had clearly imprinted themselves on our family home at 5312 Kentucky Street, and what Mom experienced was the playback on a loop. Because the house not only sits a few hundred yards from the Kanawha River, a rather muddy causeway with a brisk current, but also sits on top of an old creek system, many in my field would hypothesize that the moving water near and underneath the house contributed energy to the residual haunting.

Except, once my father's ashes were buried in late April, the activity stopped. Mom's first night at the house without the ashes was quiet and footstep-free. The quiet continued after she moved to Georgia, seven years later. This doesn't sound like a residual haunting and neither does this sound like an intelligent haunting. Why would an intelligent spirit choose to now wander a lonely cemetery rather than continue to forage for snacks in my mother's fully-stocked refrigerator?

I wondered if, in this instance, my father was visiting from a parallel universe.

I, too, thought this was a bunch of hokum. But, as a physicist, this hypothesis actually makes the most sense.

What if, on one particular day, instead of deciding to go to work, Mr. Joe Average-Guy stayed home and avoided a car accident he was supposed to cause? But what if Mr. Joe did *both* things, not only going to work and causing a three-car-pile-up, but he also stayed at home? That he did both things simultaneously? In the many-worlds interpretation, it is suggested that every single alternate history and each alternate future is real and existing alongside Joe's own history, present, and future. This hypothesis states that there is perhaps an infinite number of universes, an infinite number of Mr. Joe's, and everything that could have possibly happened in his past, but didn't, actually occurred in the past in one or more parallel universes. With this hypothesis in hand, we could say there exists a universe alongside our own where the colonies lost the Revolutionary War, where North Korea is run by a well-loved, sane, competent man who treats his citizens with respect, where George H. W. Bush not only loved broccoli, but ate it at every meal.

And, maybe, possibly, in a parallel universe, on January 28, 1998, my father called the VA and cancelled his heart catheterization procedure and rather than suffering a major heart attack during said procedure, taking blood thinners, inducing the previously-unknown brain tumor to bleed, thereby causing his untimely death? What if, in that parallel universe, he lived? And maybe, for whatever reason, the barriers between our universe and one of the universes where he survived for another three months, thinned just enough that my mother could experience the continuing midnight ritual of my father in a parallel universe?

There are so many different ideas of what paranormal activity could be and, ironically, the many-worlds interpretation is one of the more out-there explanations for those strange bumps in the night. But, for me, it is the most plausible explanation when trying to explain my father's brief post-death wanderings through my childhood West Virginia home.

How did he die in the parallel universe? Who knows? I just know that I'm extremely jealous of Parallel Universe Heather who received the gift of her father spending her 26th birthday with her and who had the benefit of her father for an extra three months. Of course, she had no way of knowing that he would pass from her existence in April, 1998, and maybe she didn't appreciate him the way she should have. But, she's not me. And, hopefully, she understood and cherished life much more than I did at that age.

Of course, Parallel Universe Heather is probably also a Nobel prize-winning physicist and that's just another reason for me to never invite her over for dinner.

CEMETERY LOVE

I grew up in South Charleston, West Virginia. Like thousands of towns across America, there's nothing special about South Charleston. Its smaller population of 12,000 compared to that of the state capital—45,000—gives it the perfect small town feel. Where it sits on the banks of the Kanawha River, it has seen tragedy and triumph, just like any town you would find on a map. But, what makes South Charleston different is that it's special to me; it was my home for 22 years. My father, as a South Charleston policeman, was firmly entrenched in the community. Coming out of the grocery store, walking to the post office, eating in a local restaurant, he would invariably be stopped by a fellow citizen to chat or they would exchange waves and salutations. I would always ask, "Who was that?" and he would seriously respond, "Not sure. I think I gave them a ticket once." Was he pulling my leg? Probably, but I could never be too sure.

The main landmark in my hometown, marking the end of D Street and sitting alongside MacCorkle Avenue, is the Criel Burial Mound. Sitting at 25-feet high, towering over everything in town except for the odd church steeple, with a pair of stone staircases on opposite sides spiraling to the top, "The Mound" was the setting for arts and crafts fairs and a perfect spot to take out-of-town guests for an elevated view of South Charleston.

As a small child, I loved racing up the railing-free stone steps. The Mound seemed infinite in its height as I would reach the top to look over my beloved town. Dad would follow me, slower and more cautiously, shouting for me to be careful. Eventually he would catch up to me at the top, watch me take in the sights of city hall, the railroad tracks at the opposite end of D Street, and the scattered houses across the Kanawha River. To me, it was just a mound of dirt, part of my infinite world of play. As I got older and better understood the history of my town, I realized that our beloved Mound was a vertical cemetery, a place where the Adena people buried their loved ones and leaders. I became concerned that I shouldn't walk on it or climb to the top because that was disrespectful to the people resting inside it. But, my father reassured me that in the 19th century, researchers from the Smithsonian came and excavated the mound, taking the skeletons and artifacts with them. I was reassured, yet still sad, that the Adena people had built this mound as a final, eternal, honored resting place for their loved ones who, instead, ended up spending eternity in a drawer somewhere in Washington, D.C.

For my family, every holiday was a chance to celebrate with food, laughter, and time together. Depending on the holiday, there would be presents, sparklers, BBQ chicken, candy, parades, and most likely no work or school. I played clarinet throughout junior high and high school, even marching in the front of the band as drum major for a few years. We would line up alongside the railroad tracks, at the far end of D Street, Mrs. Kennedy shouting for us to shut up and stand at attention. One hundred of us woodwind, brass, and percussion players, sweating in our hot polyester uniforms, would stand as still as we could, ready to help welcome whatever holiday was on the calendar. Regardless of whether it was Christmas or July 4th, veterans and beauty queens surrounded us on all sides, poised to wave to the children, fire trucks cranked up their engines with their sirens and lights at the ready. As the parade began, we would proudly head north on D Street toward the Mound, making enough noise to wake the long-dead Adena, even though they were 360 miles away in Washington, D.C. Sidewalks on both sides were filled with waving, clapping South Charlestonians shivering from the cold or sweating in the heat, depending on the season, but they were there nonetheless. When I was drum major, I took great pride in marching by myself, out front of my band, watching as the Mound grew larger as we inexorably came near. As D Street ended at the Mound, we would turn left onto 7th Avenue, end our song, and disperse in the shadow of the earthwork at the center of our hometown. My parents would find me in the crowd, and we would slowly make our way back to our car. Every holiday was a celebration, but for us it was also a remembrance of our family as we would leave the Mound and drive to the local cemetery to make sure that my paternal grandparents, Benjamin Franklin "Frank" Scarbro and Sarah "Sally" Scarbro, weren't forgotten.

Between the tiny downtown of South Charleston and my Spring Hill neighborhood sat Sunset Memorial Park where I had my first cemetery experience amongst its mix of gentle, rolling landscape, trees, mausoleums, and headstones both large and small. As a small child, I would play amongst the granite markers, blissfully unaware that I shouldn't walk on top of the graves. Dad would point out, "See there? That's where Herbert J. Thomas, Jr., is buried. He won the Congressional Medal of Honor."

I ran over to the military headstone and brushed it off, making sure there were no leaves or dirt marring the words engraved on the front. "Daddy, what is a Congressional Medal of Honor? It sounds important!"

"Well, it is," he replied, "because only the bravest soldiers get one of those."

"Did you have one?" I shouted with excitement.

"Oh, no. I don't have one, Ferntuck," he chuckled.

"I'd give you one," I pouted.

"Of course, you would." He kissed me on the head, and we made our way to my grandparents' resting place at the southwestern edge of the cemetery, just past the state senator and the town drunk off the car path. Where Frank and Sally lay is a grey, granite headstone embellished with dogwood blossoms and the surname "Scarbro" in a simple cursive.

"Daddy," I asked. "How come Gramma's and Grandpa's headstone looks different?"

"What do you mean by different?" he asked, bending down to pull a weed.

"Well," I pointed to the stone nearby, "their name is in plain letters. Gramma's and Grandpa's is pretty."

"Oh! You mean cursive!" he exclaimed, "That was your Grandpa's signature. That's how he signed his last name."

I was enthralled. As my father, mother, and Uncle Curtis tidied up the head and foot stones, placing flowers in the vases and sharing memories and stories of the people lying beneath us, I would trace my fingers along my grandfather's signature, wishing I could sit in his lap and listen to him play his fiddle or hear his stories of the coal mine like he would tell my father and uncles when they were little. I also wished I could eat my grandmother's cooking or make her smile. The pictures I saw of her reflected her hard existence, the death of her toddler daughter, and life in the coal fields where she never knew if her husband would survive another day of mining coal. I always believed that if I could spend an hour with her, I would make her giggle, her face lighting up with a rare smile.

After the requisite number of minutes it took to exchange out the flowers and make sure their graves looked tended, we would leave until the next holiday or visiting Scarbro family member arrived when we would make the trek back to hold vigil and remember. Whenever we would drive by Sunset Memorial Park, which was several times a week, I would always look over in the direction of my grandparents' resting place and feel guilty that I was still alive without them.

As I grew up, I moved away from tradition, feeling annoyed that I had to remember the dead. Why should I be concerned about death when I had so much living to do? College with its sorority socials, dorm life, and young people everywhere allowed me to forget about death and its inevitability. Visiting any cemetery only served to fuel my anxieties and fears. It was much easier to ignore the dead and dying, and spend as much time as possible living and being around my friends who reminded me, daily, that we were young and vibrant. During my college years and 20s, I never stepped foot in any cemetery. Scarce visits home didn't include trips to Sunset Memorial Park. I would drive by and make sure to look straight ahead whenever we passed, never allowing my eyes to trail over to the quiet headstones and the guilt I knew would inevitably follow.

After marrying Tyler and permanently settling in suburban Atlanta, I took in my new home and gradually acclimated myself to the differences between depressed Appalachia and the sprawling metropolis of Atlanta. Where the population of West Virginia was declining, Atlanta was booming. Here, houses were being built as fast as possible, front yards looking more like giant, green quilts because the sod squares hadn't yet taken root. After our wedding and moving into our first home, I finally stuck my head up for air, looked around, and couldn't find the cemeteries. Even though I was still terrified of death, I had become fascinated with cemeteries, and I wondered why I never saw any. And then, it dawned on me that most modern cemeteries near my new home were built for function, not personality. These newfangled cemeteries consisted of perfectly manicured lawns interspersed with ground-level granite markers that lay flush with the grass. Here, it was the convenience of modern-day landscaping that trumped the artistry of stonemasons who could carve personal sentiments into granite, gifting the living with words from the dead. Flying by on the four-lane, I could spot flags dotting the landscape during patriotic holidays and a few plastic flowers, but the following week en route to pick up the kids,

I would sigh with frustration when I would see a cloud of dust swirling as landscape workers removed flowers and flags from the graves, while others mowed the grass and blew away the leaves. I decided right then that I would never be buried in such a sanitized, forgetful way. Clearly, we, as a society, had become more interested in convenience than in creating a contemplative space for our living relatives.

It wasn't until several years after our marriage that I discovered Oakland Cemetery. Located in downtown Atlanta, it's a beautiful Victorian-era garden cemetery, 48 acres in the center of an otherwise cold, concrete jungle. I was stunned by the park-like atmosphere with paths winding underneath century-old oak trees, grand statuary around every corner, and benches for quiet contemplation. I loved that I could take inspiration from author Margaret Mitchell while sitting beside her grave, quietly relax near the private spot under an old oak tree where Atlanta's first black mayor, Maynard Jackson, chose to rest, and giggle at the perfect putting green covering golfer Bobby Jones's grave site with golf balls left by his adoring fans scattered on the perfectly manicured grass. My first time there, I wandered through a sea of Confederate soldiers, explored the close confines of Jewish headstones, unable to decipher the Hebrew words carved on their tall markers, and touched elaborate family mausoleums covered in gargoyles and Egyptian lotus flowers. In Oakland, there are grand oak trees shading quiet paved pathways, graves that resemble beds with marble pillows that look soft but are hard to the touch, beautiful flowers spilling around angels and cherubs, and even a small granite lamb that marks the final resting place of a child's pet bird. In fact, I've spent many an hour roaming the paths of Oakland, taking pictures, enjoying the quiet—until a police siren screams in the distance—wondering where I would put my mausoleum.

In Oakland, I don't fear death. I actively think about it and the beauty there can be in passing on. When I see the sanitized cemeteries of the suburbs, I see only loneliness and grief, the dead resting alone with no one to walk amongst their beds of grass. At Oakland, I can touch the beautiful stonemasonry, take refuge from the brutal Georgia summer sun in the shade of a living canopy, and meet Atlanta families who helped found the city I now call home. At Oakland cemetery, death no longer is a thing to fear, but an old friend to someday embrace.

I have a favorite mausoleum I like to visit whenever I'm at Oakland, and as I peer into the padlocked, iron doors, gazing at the serene stained glass windows within, I fantasize about the mausoleum I would build for my own family. It would be a gaudy, gargoyle-encrusted, art deco, Egyptian hieroglyph monstrosity that could serve as the final resting place for not just the Dobsons, but for many of our friends. The Dobson-Livingston-Sammons-Brown-Garner-Murphy mausoleum has yet to be built, but I have high hopes that it will become the centerpiece of whatever cemetery in which we choose to build it. It won't be a place for our children to plant us and forget. It will revive the park-like atmosphere of cemeteries past and encourage our families to come back and visit each holiday and birthday, sharing flowers and decorations like my parents and uncle did at Sunset Memorial Park.

Alongside the Sunset Memorial Parks and the Oaklands of the world, there are the cemeteries with no names, no grand design, and no caretakers. It's in these nearly-forgotten places that a handful of professionally-carved headstones sit next to small, hand-carved stones. Some families could only leave a pile of rocks to mark the final resting place of their loved one while others had nothing, the person's final resting place eventually being lost to time and nature. Here, the perpetual care exists only on the backs of those living family members who bring their landscaping tools and muscles. It's in these cemeteries that headstones come in all shapes and sizes and typically disappear underneath nature's detritus and ever-encroaching ivy. My father and uncle are buried in such a cemetery. On the West Virginia Turnpike, between the Morton Travel Plaza and exit 66, is an access road. Beside that road, on the side of the mountain, overlooking Paint Creek, is Greencastle Cemetery, one of those overgrown, quiet places full of the dead loved ones of local coal mining families. The privately-owned house that marked the cemetery's location has since burned down, and the only proof of the cemetery's existence is a small green road sign a few feet before the turn off.

When I visit Greencastle, I never go alone because the bears are numerous and the poison ivy is plentiful. Some families have marked their plots with chain-link fences, others with low brick borders. Straight up the hill and to the left is the Scarbro family plot where numerous cousins and my grandfather's brother are buried, several taken by a spinal meningitis outbreak that occurred after the 1932 Paint Creek flood. My Aunt Clorine, whose childhood home was carried away in the flood, recalls seeing her siblings' bodies transported away on the train. Back then, there weren't funeral homes in the rural areas to tend to the dead. Families washed and prepared the bodies of their loved ones at home. To keep the outbreak from spreading any further, the authorities took away Aunt Clorine's siblings and sent them to a funeral home in Charleston. Later, they returned home in coffins, ready for burial. Clorine's parents weren't allowed to open the coffins, not allowed to view their children one last time, as to do so could have meant death for them. Our family's small plot consists of a few granite headstones, a tree in one corner, and much care and love. It's not much, but it's the final home of my family. I never even knew of the cemetery's existence until my father and uncle's deaths.

In April, 1998, three months after their deaths, it was time to put my father's and uncle's remains to rest. After witnessing the sanitized cemeteries of Georgia and knowing my mother couldn't afford mausoleum spots at Sunset Memorial, I decided to scatter their ashes in places of note. But the Scarbro first cousins all protested. They wanted a burial site to visit, clean, mow, and take care of. So, I acquiesced and on that hillside near Paint Creek, I stood amongst those family headstones, looking for the perfect spot. All of my first cousins-once removed—being from West Virginia, you've got to know all this first-, second-, third-cousins once-, twice-, thrice-removed stuff so that you know who it's okay to marry—were standing around, waiting on me. There was Clorine, her husband Deskar, Violet and her husband Mike. My mom stood next to me and in my arms were the boxes containing Dad's and Uncle Curtis's ashes. Everything felt wrong in that moment because rather than holding them, they should have been holding me. I had cried most of the drive over, knowing that putting them in the ground was truly the end. Before leaving that morning, with Mom's encouragement, I had spooned out a small bit of Dad's ashes and put them in a locket. I was determined to carry a small part of Dad with me wherever I went.

As I looked around, my red, puffy eyes rested on the perfect spot. It was at the upper corner of the plot, under the tree. I pointed there and said, "That's where I want to bury them."

Violet replied, "Oh, you can't bury them there. Penny's leg is there. After she was hit by that car and the doctors cut it off, we buried it there."

I looked at Violet, my mouth open, and asked, "Seriously? You buried Penny's leg?"

She responded in the only way she could. "Yeah. We didn't want to lose it."

For the first three months after my father's and uncle's deaths, I really didn't laugh. I was mired in sadness and a deep depression. But, in that moment, in that tiny, overgrown cemetery on a forgotten West Virginia hillside cradling my beloved Dad and Uncle, I busted out into laughter. Tears poured from my eyes, and I doubled over, falling to my knees, laughing so hard that I had to gasp for breath before doing it again.

"Holy crap! You *buried* her *LEG?!*"

They all looked at me like I was crazy. At least Mike let out a small chuckle.

Eventually, though, they couldn't help it, and Violet's raspy laughter and Clorine's loud guffaws joined in. Even Mom was snorting. I, meanwhile, could barely function. After a few minutes of cathartic mirth,

I wiped my face and took several deep breaths, avoiding glancing at Penny's leg's final resting place, knowing that if I even looked over in that direction, I would lose it again. I glanced at the fence line, my great uncle's headstone, and then looked down at the corner opposite cousin Penny's appendage. I knew that that was the perfect spot, large enough for both their boxes and headstones, and right next to the gate. Mike began digging and soon enough, there were two holes. I placed their ashes, boxes and all, inside and Mike covered them up. It was done. Dad and Uncle Curtis were buried. We hugged each other, wept a few more tears, and slowly, we left.

A few months later, their headstones were delivered, and my last remaining uncle supervised their installation. Now, whenever I make the trek to West Virginia, I visit their graves. I take three roses: one for Dad, one for Uncle Curtis, and one for Penny's leg. Penny died several years ago and they didn't reunite her with her leg. The rest of her is buried about 15 miles away, next to her husband, in Montgomery, West Virginia. I love visiting with Dad and Uncle Curtis because I will inevitably walk up the slight hill to Penny's leg, place her rose on the ground, and begin talking to it.

"Hey there, Penny's leg! Just wanted to let you know that the rest of you passed away a few years back. Sorry they didn't reunite you. Anyway, let me tell you about the kids…"

Death is an inexorable part of life. And so are cemeteries. We decorate our homes to match our personalities, to convey visual messages about our lives in the hopes that visitors will attain a better understanding of who we are. For the families who do that and the cemeteries that allow it, the final resting places become celebrations of the lives that were led, the loves that were cherished, and the families who came after. Cemeteries are about remembrance. They are places for the living. Here, away from my big city in my little hometown with its Native American burial mound to a mountain once full of coal, now dotted with dead miners, I feel cemeteries are gathering places for the living, keeping us humble. Where will I end up? I have no idea. But, wherever it is, I hope it's in the biggest, gaudiest mausoleum on the block, with a disembodied leg nearby to keep me company.

THE SWINGING
CHANDELIER

As the 1990s began to wane, I had one thing, and one thing only, on my mind. I wanted a Mazda Miata. Ever since my college days when one of my sorority sisters came home from summer vacation with a cute little red Miata with a black rag top, I knew I had to have one. This itch was made worse during my technical writing years when I found myself as a Senior Course Developer at ExecuTrain, and one of my fellow writers showed up one day with a black Miata with a tan top and manual transmission. It was love at first sight. I would constantly pester her to let me drive it. I would park my bland white Honda Civic next to her beautiful black Miata, and when we would go out to lunch, I would offer to drive her car, to "give her a break," assuring her of my abilities to not burn out her clutch. Thankfully, my dear father, in a fit of "Got to keep my little girl safe!" had taught me how to drive a stick shift. At the time, I thought he was addled.

"Why?! Why do I have to learn how to do this?! Everyone has automatic cars! Nobody drives stick shifts! This is stupid!" I would cry.

Dad's calm response was always, "Because if you get in trouble and the only car available to you is a stick shift, then you'll be able to drive it when no one else can."

Of course, he never explained why the mysterious owner of this stick shift car couldn't just drive it himself and why it would solely be up to me to drive this manual transmission car. He also never specified what kind of trouble, but for him, his logic was sound. And so I learned how to drive stick shift behind the wheel Dad's extremely temperamental, canary-yellow Chevette. It was the tiniest of cars, slightly larger than a Yugo, and only went up to fourth gear. To put it in reverse, I had to mash down on the gear head, shove it into neutral, and push it to the left and back. Half the time, when I would stop at a light, I would forget to put it in first gear and spend the next five minutes, crying and screaming as the cars behind me relentlessly honked their horns, all because the damned thing would stall out while I tried to start it from a stop in fourth gear. That Chevette and I hated each other. Eventually, though, we formed a truce, much like the Korean War Armistice and worked together with little to no trust.

My all-encompassing need to possess my own Miata pushed me to take a second job. Toni, who was then the manager for the local real estate magazine, needed someone to color-correct house photos taken by hapless real estate agents. I would spend seven evenings each month at a small office in downtown Cumming, mastering Photoshop on a Mac. It was a fun year of work, and I got to know the magazine's owners, John and Pam, as well Pam's mother Rose.

Rose was a master potter who made the most beautiful pots and vases, glazing them with a special technique called raku. After a metallic glaze was applied to the piece, it was fired a second time and then left in the open air. Sometimes, water was applied to the pottery and that caused the glaze to crackle. I was honored to spend several Saturday afternoons over the course of a year, helping Rose transfer pieces from the kiln to the open air. Many times, we would speed up the cooling and cracking process with water from the garden hose. Pam would make us lemonade, and we would all oooh and aaah at every piece that came out of the kiln. In love with Rose's talent, I bought several pieces for my family's home.

Not long after I finished my year-long job with the magazine, I purchased my dream car—a 1999 silver Miata with black soft top and, of course, a manual transmission. Soon after, John died very suddenly and unexpectedly. Devastated, Pam and Rose came to depend more on each other for companionship. I remember Pam saying that she and her mother had long talks about death, promising one another that whoever died first would try to communicate with the one still living. Within a few years, Rose began suffering from dementia and was later confined to a wheelchair. Before she passed away, Toni, Pam, and I fired her final few pots as Rose looked on. We tried to decipher her "glaze cookbook" but were unsuccessful. Rose was confused and couldn't remember what she had written or why. That final day of firing in the sunshine was bittersweet.

After Rose passed, we gathered at the local funeral home for her service. It was your typical big box funeral home with neutral chapels and viewing rooms, all very quiet and tastefully decorated. In the largest of the chapels was Rose's coffin, closed and covered with a gorgeous, colorful spray of flowers. As an artist, she would have gotten a kick out of the many shades represented in those blooms. There was a set of pews on each side of a center aisle, each with a large brass chandelier centered overhead. Toni and I sat next to one another near the back of the room, listening to the eulogy and the kind words that family, friends, and local artists had to say about Rose. At the end, Pam approached the lectern to speak.

As soon as Pam began talking, the very large chandelier nearest to her began to sway side-to-side, slowly at first but then gradually picking up height and speed. Toni and I immediately noticed it and ribbed each other with our elbows. We watched, wide-eyed, as this chandelier swung back and forth, as if controlled by ropes and pulleys. We waited, breathlessly, for it to fall into the crowd or to crack the ceiling. I honestly don't remember what Pam said about Rose because I was too busy watching the actions of the chandelier. As Pam's brief words came to a close, the light fixture slowed its movements and stopped as soon as Pam took her seat. Toni and I looked at one another, in shock, over the events of the last several minutes. As soon as the ceremony was over, we bolted out to the lobby and tracked down the nearest employee.

"Hi there!" I brightly asked, "Are you one of the funeral directors?"

"Yes, I am," he replied. "Can I help you with something?"

"Absolutely," Toni piped in. "Is this place haunted?"

The look on his face was rather comical. He coughed and sputtered and finally replied, "Not really."

Toni and I looked at each other knowingly and returned to the chapel. We looked all around for air vents, and when we didn't see any near the chandelier, we looked around for wires or fishing line, convinced it was a scam. When we couldn't find any logical reason for the chandelier's movement, we left for Pam's house. As we drove away in my Miata, Toni piped up.

"What the hell?"

"I have no idea," I replied. "That was just nuts."

"I know, right?" Toni said, astonished. "I mean, we both saw that. You saw that, right?"

"Oh," I said, "I totally saw that."

"And it couldn't have been a vent."

"There wasn't a vent anywhere around it!" I exclaimed "And even if there were, that thing was too big to get pushed around by an HVAC system."

"No, you're right," she said, "and we've so got to tell Pam."

"Oh, heck yeah we do," I replied.

Once at Pam's house for the wake, we cornered her.

"Please," Toni said, "please tell me you saw the chandelier moving while you were talking about your mom!"

"Yes, Pam!" replied a neighbor. "I saw it too! Did you see it?"

"What do you mean the chandelier was moving?" Pam asked, confused. "I didn't see anything except the piece of paper I was reading off of."

"You're kidding," Toni said. "The whole time you were talking, the chandelier above you was swinging! And as soon as you sat down, it stopped!"

Pam was shocked. "It must have been Mom! We promised each other that we would make our presence known when we died. It had to have been her!"

Over the ten years since Rose's passing, I move around from room to room in my house, taking inspiration from different writing spots. Whenever I'm in my family room, I can see several of Rose's raku pots on my shelves. Black, cream, green, and silver, all with their signature cracked, metallic glaze glinting in the lights, they remind me of those sun-dappled afternoons, drinking lemonade beside a hot kiln, excitement in our voices as we waited to see what color her clay creations would take. I sometimes wonder if Rose wanders my home, her connections to her creations so strong that she visits them from time to time. I like to think she's here, watching over my writing just as I watched over her clay creations. She hasn't made her presence known, but I'm so thankful for the parting gift she gave us that day at the funeral home, and I'm grateful, too, for taking that job with the 400 North Real Estate Guide and getting to know her, along with Pam and John. It was one of the best decisions I ever made.

Today, I drive a very sensible automatic minivan. The flashiest thing about it is its 12 cup holders. Whenever I drive the kids to school or I make a grocery store run, I'll see someone driving a cute silver Miata, and I'll remember those three years with fondness and ache. I know it was the logical thing to do, trading in that fun, sporty car for a practical family car, but I've always regretted letting it go. Sometimes, I think about getting the top of the minivan cut off and replaced with a soft top. Or, maybe all it needs is a little raku pot sitting on the dashboard to remind me of my carefree, childless, convertible days.

PERCHANCE
TO DREAM

"Heather, do you think they'll ever prove the existence of aliens?" he would ask me.

"I don't know, Dad. But, the Universe is a pretty big place, and it would be selfish to think we're the only ones in it."

"I think you're right. All those people who have seen aliens can't be wrong," he would say with a smile.

Tom Scarbro was probably one of the main reasons I became a paranormal investigator. My father, even with his high school education, was curious about the world around him, and we would engage in these discussions quite frequently. As my love for science fiction—and heck, just plain science—grew, we would talk more and more about the unexplained. Like any other dad, he guided me, protected me, argued with me, embarrassed me, and loved me unconditionally. He never came right out and said, "I believe in ghosts and UFOs and chupacabras!" but his constant questioning of the world around him made me believe that a part of him was curious and wanted to know more about that unknown world just out of our reach.

When I look back on all the intervening years since Dad's death, thinking about the things I've done and accomplished since our paths so severely veered, I am most saddened that he isn't here to be with his grandchildren, on whom I know he would dote and spoil. I also wish he were here to investigate the paranormal with me. I imagine we would have long, late-night conversations about all of the investigations I've been on, the interesting people I've met, and the experiences I've had. I know he would avidly listen to every word and add his own intriguing opinions and ideas.

"Really? You heard a voice that shouldn't be there?" he would ask.

"Yes! It was all of us girls in the room, there weren't any men! Jordan and Clint were outside! So, explain to me how come there's a man's voice answering Nancy's question?" I would excitedly reply.

"Well, I don't know. Can I hear it?" he would respond.

"Sure! I'll email it to you. Get Mom to help you open and play the file." And I would sit on pins and needles waiting for his response. Would he go on an investigation with me? I have no idea. That question will never be answered.

The one thing I've been too fearful to do on an investigation is try to contact him. Whenever I sit in a client's home, I'm there for the client. I'm there to talk to whatever spirit is in their home and try to answer the question, "Why are you here?" I've never been brave enough to turn on my audio recorder in my own home to see if my father would respond because I think it would sadden me if he did. It would mean that he feels that he needs to come back and check on me and still be a parent, rather than enjoying his afterlife. But, I know that he returned, at least once, to visit my dreams.

In many different religious communities, the faithful believe newly-departed souls linger nearby for a short while after their passing and that experiencing your loved one during that time is not uncommon. For example, the Greek Orthodox believe the soul lingers on Earth for three days before moving on. I wasn't raised Greek Orthodox, but I do think there could be something to this idea of the dead remaining close to the familiar, not just before moving on, but also at any time after their death. As a former Presbyterian, I can tell you that at least one Bible verse sticks out in my head when I think of my father. It's John 14:2 and it states, "In my Father's house there are many mansions: if it were not so, I would have told you. I go to prepare a place for you." This wasn't his favorite verse but it reminds me of the dream I had shortly after he died, when he may have been hesitant to leave us.

In this dream, I found myself walking down a street much like those on which I rode my bicycle as a child. It was concrete, rough and cracked from the weight of many cars passing over its surface, and just wide enough to allow for parked cars on either side and one car to drive down the middle. As I walked down this street, I saw homes that looked like those in a typical South Charleston, West Virginia, neighborhood. They were small, one-story houses with aluminum siding and neat, postage-stamp yards. I approached one as if I lived there, even though I had never seen this house before in my waking life. I walked through the front door, took a left into the well-decorated living room, and there sat my father, dressed to the nines in a very stylish suit and tie. As soon as he saw me, he stood up, walked over to me, took up my right hand with his left, placed his right hand at my waist, and we danced a waltz. There was no music, just sunlight, peace, and joy at seeing my father again. And we looked at each other and just danced.

And then I woke up.

Why do I think my father actually visited me in a dream rather than it just being my subconscious trying to grasp at straws? Because this was so out-of-character for both of us. My father didn't dance except to do, as Billy Crystal called it, "the white man's overbite," and my dancing was of the 1980s "electrocuted white girl" nature. Neither of us had ever waltzed, and any dream my subconscious made up would have involved the familiarity of our smart-ass conversations that always ended in him saying, "And may the Force be with you!" and then laughter. This is why I believe people when they tell me about dreaming of their departed loved ones. I don't discount it because whether it's a true visitation or not, it is certainly healing.

Twice more, my dad came to me. Seven years after he died, when I was going through infertility treatments, he visited me again in my dreams, this time bringing Uncle Curtis along for the ride. They asked me how I was doing, and I unloaded on both of them. I complained about having to inject myself with fertility drugs, how I couldn't eat the sugary snacks I so loved, and I lamented that the whole process was invasive and stole any semblance of humanity from me. I cried that I had gone through this four separate times with no luck and that I was tired and ready to adopt. They nodded, listened, and comforted me. I don't remember our dream conversation, but the gist of it was that whatever I decided to do, adoption or fertility treatments, they supported me and loved me no matter what. Several days later, I was artificially inseminated for the fifth and final time. I would be pregnant with Amelia and Heath just two short weeks later.

The last visit was during a period in my life when I felt everything was hopeless and I was experiencing anxiety and panic that I could no longer control. My chemical imbalances could no longer be ignored, and I was in the middle of a two-week long panic attack that had me wondering if my heart would finally give out like Dad's. It was at the end of those two weeks when I paid a visit to my doctor and begged her for help. We talked, she hugged me, and I practically ran to the pharmacy, anti-depression and anti-anxiety prescriptions in hand. When I returned home, I lay down in my bed and tried to tell myself that it was all going to be okay. Suddenly, I felt a hand brush across my forehead. Lynda Carter was on the TV screen, saving the world in her red, white, and blue Amazon uniform, and my dog and cat were sleeping in other rooms. I was completely alone. Or was I? I know I felt a hand, comforting me, and I know that I felt utter peace in the moments immediately after. I knew right then that everything would be just fine.

My mother was witness to my father's late-night snack wanderings for those three months after his passing. I didn't witness any of my father's roving during my visits home, but I do truly believe that he has visited me in the years since. My dreams and the fleeting moment of comfort are as much a part of my memories of him as those made while he was living. They are precious to me, and I'll never forget how wonderfully we danced together.

A FIRST TIME
FOR EVERYTHING

It was a cold, crisp February evening, and I was a mix of nervousness, excitement, and bloat. I squeezed myself into a pair of jeans that were one size too small, having given birth to Jarrod just nine months before and refusing to buy new clothes. I searched around for my nicest black sweater, looked in the mirror and put on mascara and lipstick, determined not to look as tired and old as I felt. Having three children, all under the age of three, kept me in a perpetual state of fatigue, but I was determined to learn everything I could about investigating the paranormal. Acceptance into Atlanta Paranormal Investigations had come easy, but I knew that to keep my place, I would have to make myself invaluable. I had read the small instruction manual that came with my digital voice recorder, and I tightly gripped my small flashlight with its fresh AA batteries. I was ready and yet I wasn't. I was terrified that I was going to be found lacking at this new phase of my life, and I was worried that if something paranormal interacted with me, I would react negatively and run away from this opportunity.

I didn't want to fail.

As I said goodbye to my family, Tyler wished me good luck. Amelia, Heath, and Jarrod, too young to understand what was going on, gamely accepted my kisses and hugs and immediately went back to playing with their toys. Soon, they would go to bed, oblivious to their mother standing in the dark with a bunch of strangers, talking to the air around them. As they slept, I would investigate.

When I arrived at the J. Christopher's restaurant in Roswell, Georgia, I was joined by the other newly minted investigators-in-training, all new members of Darlene's team. Ranging in ages and sizes, we all rooted through our small equipment bags, trying to look busy, each of us feeling awkward because, even though we were being driven by the same purpose, we were strangers to one another. Standing around making small talk was Clint, the fireman-EMT, Stefanie, the college student, Jordan, the other college student, Steve, the electrician, Tammy, the high school teacher, and Darlene, our leader, along with a smattering of others.

I had run out of things to add to the conversation and, standing there, I felt tired and terrified all at the same time. I wondered if the ghosts in this building were hiding away or if they were already surrounding us, listening in on our conversations, our deepest thoughts, deciding if we were worthy enough to see and hear them. I also wondered if Darlene would fully accept me into the group after that night. She and her husband, the group's founders, had hinted that they were interested in working this group into an outlet for a TV show, and I knew I wasn't much to look at. Even if I did well with the investigation, would they want someone of my age and physicality in their group? Would that even matter? Fingers crossed, I took a deep breath and began the journey of a lifetime.

As we stood in the dining area, the lingering smells of bacon, waffles, and coffee assaulted my nose. It was a divine smell, and I vowed to revisit this breakfast-themed restaurant another day while they were open. Darlene told us a brief history of the building. Once called The Public House, it was built in 1854 and served as the commissary for the textile mill in Roswell, Georgia. Over the decades, it had been a general store for The Roswell Mill's workers, a shoe shop, a funeral home, and several restaurants. During the Civil War, General Sherman spared the building and used it as a Union Army hospital. Allegedly, Southern belle and nurse Catherine fell in love with Union soldier Michael and, as the story goes, when he was killed by Confederate soldiers, she died of a broken heart. This is an apocryphal story, passed down through the decades, that many Roswell residents have accepted as fact.

We were gathered at The Public House / J. Christopher's that night for a training investigation and to hopefully capture evidence of Michael and Catherine still haunting the building. As I listened to Darlene, I looked out the front windows of the restaurant toward the square. People were briskly walking to and from local dinner restaurants, bars, and their cars, bundled up to avoid the winter chill. I wondered if they could see me in this darkened window and if they were even aware of the rich history surrounding them. In that moment, I vowed to keep my head down, do what I was told, and come out the other side of this investigation a valued member of the group. Unlike my sorority, honor clubs, and college alumnae groups where I had felt the need to lead and be the decision maker, here I merely wanted acceptance and answers. I would be happy to be labeled, "Heather Dobson, Just an Investigator."

Darlene divided us into several small groups, and we began to roam the building in sections. One group visited the extremely haunted women's bathroom, another headed for the equipment room in the attic, while a third group, my group, investigated the common area of the second floor. As the breakfast smells continued to linger, Clint, Stefanie, Jordan, Steve, Tammy, and I nervously put our game faces on. My senses were heightened, and every shuffle or fleeting shadow drew my immediate attention. As my doubts and nervousness melted away and were replaced by the thrill of the unknown, I became very aware of my surroundings. I felt like I could see and hear everything. As I moved from location to location, firmly grasping my new recorder and flashlight, asking questions aloud of whatever was there and hoping for an answer, I felt the allure of what I was doing. I was actually in an honest-to-goodness haunted building, in the dark, in the middle of the night, with a bunch of like-minded people. The exhilaration was palpable.

Toward the end of the investigation, sometime well after midnight, we all gathered for one final session in the upstairs equipment room. Our recorders at the ready, we asked questions hoping something was answering in the form of an electronic voice phenomena. An EVP is a sound that is interpreted as a spirit's voice on an audio recording. When the audio recording is reviewed, either immediately or days or weeks after the investigation, if there are any unexplainable voices that can't be attributed to the investigators who were present at the time of the recording, then we assume it is the recording of a disembodied spirit voice, sometimes directly answering our questions, sometimes not. The electromagnetic field (EMF) meters a few people carried were recording a high electromagnetic field thanks to the breaker box, furnace, and various other pieces of equipment that helped to run the restaurant below. Not only could this extremely high EMF attract spirits, as they could siphon off this extra energy to manifest, it caused me to feel a literal buzz.

I walked into that room with my nervous and heightened senses, coupled with EMF-induced light-headedness. I took my place in the back of the group, in the back of the room with no one behind me, practically drunk on the moment, with my eyes glued to the doorway where moonlight added a glow to the equipment and my fellow investigators. I tried to will a shadow to materialize or a voice to echo. I yearned for a moment so startling that it would change my life forever. But, nothing happened. The night ended, for me, without so much as a whispered, "Hello."

I drove home in a stupor, hungover from the adrenaline high and exhaustion. I decided that even though I hadn't heard a knock like Stefanie or felt a touch like Clint, that maybe it was because I was too tired, too nervous. Maybe, rather than showing themselves to me, the spirits of Catherine and Michael instead spoke into my voice recorder, giving me a gift to be found and savored later. Eventually, I arrived home to the hall light Tyler had so thoughtfully left on. I peeked in my children's rooms, watched their chests lightly rise and fall, peaceful in their dreams. I eventually slid into my warm bed and drifted off to sleep, curled next to my husband, surrounded by love, but alone in my thoughts.

I spent the next week listening to my audio files for a total of ten hours—five hours straight from the recorder and then a full repeat after I enhanced the audio—and the more I listened, the more despondent I became. Nothing spoke. I downloaded the files from the recorder to my computer and listened to them there. Still, nothing. I smashed my headphones against my ears and turned up the volume, trying desperately to hear something, anything, that wasn't my voice or the voices of my fellow investigators. Except, there were no disembodied whispers tucked between the white noise of the living. I felt betrayed, like I had been found unworthy by the dead to ask their purpose.

I begrudgingly sent my report to Darlene, letting her know that I had discovered no EVPs and that I hadn't experienced anything out of the ordinary. Nothing had touched me, spoken to me, or appeared before me. I wondered if this whole endeavor was an empty mistake. Darlene assured me that she hadn't captured any evidence her first time on an investigation either. This made me feel a little bit better, but I was still disappointed.

When we gathered at that same J. Christopher's for our monthly meeting, Darlene pulled out her computer so that we could all listen to the EVPs from the training investigations. Everyone began chattering with excitement.

"Were you in the bathroom when we heard the knock on the wall?" Tammy asked.

"Yes!" Clint replied. "It was so loud! I captured a voice in the basement."

"And then something touched my shoulder when we were in the basement," Stefanie replied.

My face fell because I had nothing to contribute. So, I quietly sipped my coffee, listened to the excitement around me, and hoped no one would ask what evidence I had captured. Again, I was alone. I looked upward, staring at the very ceiling that supported Michael and Catherine's second level dance floor, wondering if at that very moment they were watching and still finding me unworthy. I decided in that instant that I would continue on this journey, no matter the results. Even a lack of evidence is still evidence when looking from a scientific angle. I would model myself as an invaluable member of the group, one with a science background, a skeptical mind, and a willingness to learn, even in the face of no evidence or personal experiences. I glanced back up, saluted the ceiling with my coffee mug, and joined the conversations of the living going on around me.

I've heard it said the first time you do anything is the best, and after that, the newness wears off and the thrill that runs up your spine slowly numbs and is replaced with experience. Investigating the paranormal is the same way. If I find myself at a new location, the thrill returns, but only slightly. No investigation, no night, will ever compare to that first time standing in the Roswell Public House, at the edge of the cliff, ready to jump off into oblivion. I'm still soaring, though, arms spread wide, exploring the unknown landscape before me, but I now do it with a practiced eye and a bit of cynicism, wishing I could recapture that first night of absolute clarity.

QUIET AS MICE

Our first real investigation, where we trainees would stay up all night, have complete access to a property, and would finally be full-fledged investigators with official shirts and everything—seriously, we were pumped!—was at Gaither Plantation in Covington, Georgia. The stately home and land, owned by the Gaither family from 1850 through the next century, stood witness to slavery, the Civil War, hidden Confederate soldiers, and possibly murder. On the drive south, I couldn't shut up. I jabbered away like a nervous felon in the back of Clint's minivan.

In addition to standing as Newton County's premier historical site, Gaither Plantation was also a location where many couples held their dream nuptials. The two-story, white farmhouse was a beautiful backdrop for weddings and family reunions, while inside, amidst the 19th-century period furniture, bridal parties could change into their wedding finery and relax before the big moment or families could escape the heat—literal and figural—of gatherings. Near the large house stood several buildings that were the old slave quarters, and further along the dirt road stood a church. Behind the house, along a path through the woods, was the old family cemetery. It was exciting to think that we would have permission to explore and investigate the entire property.

The farmhouse was beautiful, and we were careful to step around the old furniture. Much of it was original to the house, and even though we were welcome here, we didn't want to damage anything. At the rear of the home in the old parlor amidst the century-old chairs and the more modern sofas, we found the home for our base camp. This was where we set up our digital video recorder and computer monitor, as well as run all the cables from our infrared cameras. We placed our late-night snacks and thermoses of coffee in the nearby kitchen and waited for Darlene to divide us into smaller groups.

Throughout our multiple training investigations, I discovered that I was older than many members of our group. Stefanie was barely in her 20s, single, and in college. Steve was 28, single, and working as an electrician. Here I was, an old lady of her late-30s with three kids. Some nights when I would sit and talk to them on investigations, I realized how out of touch I had become with modern American culture. Hidden away with my young children, I barely left the house. Atlanta Paranormal Investigations had become a sort of social outlet for me. Stefanie, in particular, amazed me with her drive and creativity while Steve, a gruff Michigander on the outside, was quiet and introspective once you looked within. They both had a keen sense of humor, and Stefanie, in particular, dragged me kicking and screaming into the 21st century by sending me my first ever text in 2008. Once I began texting my fellow paranormal investigators, I didn't stop and it was all Stefanie's fault. So, when Darlene told Stefanie, Steve, and I, that we would be investigating together as a team, I was thrilled.

Each group, in turn, roamed around different areas of the property. While one group investigated the farm house, another would be at the slave quarters, a third would investigate the cemetery, and the fourth would sit at base camp and watch the video display, as well as monitor communications with walkie-talkies. Watching the infrared camera feed allowed us to keep track of all the investigators and to make note of any strange anomalies caught on the cameras. The holy grail of paranormal evidence is the appearance of a ghost on camera.

When it came time for Stefanie, Steve, and I to monitor base camp, our eyes were glued to the computer screen, carefully watching all the cameras for any evidence of a ghost popping up to say, "Howdy y'all!" While the other teams settled in to their various locations inside and outside the house, testing their walkie-talkies, the three of us grabbed coffee and snacks, ready for a long couple of hours in the dark with a glowing monitor for company. Next to us was a room housing a grand piano and behind us was the comfortable furniture for bridal parties. We chose to sit in the metal folding chairs because any comfort this late in the game would certainly cause us to fall asleep. The room across the hall was decorated as a 19th century children's nursery, and Stefanie's first order of business was to cover the ceramic baby doll with a blanket because, as Stefanie stated quite matter-of-factly, "All dolls are possessed." Neither Steve nor I argued with her because, honestly, the damned thing did look pretty creepy, and I knew that if I looked into the room and saw its head move, I would break some Gaither family treasures to be the first one out the front door. The other teams radioed to us that they had begun their EVP sessions, and we silently watched their progress from our station.

Within 15 minutes, the radio crackled and Darlene, who was investigating with her team upstairs, asked us what we were doing. We responded that we were sitting and watching. She reported that she was hearing loud noises from our location. We were baffled. Except for the quiet hum of our equipment and intermittent slurp of coffee, there was no noise. This continued several times throughout the shift. Each time she radioed downstairs that she could hear us making too much noise, we would vehemently deny even breathing loudly.

It became so ridiculous that the three of us barely moved. I, of course, being the clumsy one of the group, tried to quietly shift in my chair, managing to drop my potato chip bag. Stefanie and Steve immediately rounded on me with fingers to lips and accusatory stares made pale by the sickly green light of the computer display. We had lived in fear of this moment, not because we were new, but because Darlene had reminded us many, many, many... *many* times over the last few months that people were lined up to join our group and that we could be replaced at any time with someone more eager than ourselves. Stefanie, Steve, and I knew, viscerally, that if we screwed up here, at this historic site, we would never have another opportunity to explore the paranormal. It was bad enough that we sat in fear in an old, dark home, waiting for the proverbial ghost to jump out and shout, "Boo!" but to also sit in fear of the living was beginning to grind on our good graces. As the shift waned, and Darlene's communication with us had finally quieted, something—or someone—struck one of the keys of the grand piano in the room next to us. As one, our heads whipped in the direction of the piano and, after a pause, we looked at each other, mouths gaping, holding our collective breath, waiting for Darlene to accuse us of playing the piano, but the radio stayed silent. Thankfully, we were able to enjoy that moment without accusation.

As the shift ended, the other groups from outside trickled in, and Darlene and her team finally made it downstairs. She proceeded to tell us that the noise they heard from upstairs was loud, as if the three of us were downstairs, having a party. The rest of her team corroborated her story, and we could do nothing but shrug our shoulders and answer wide-eyed, "It wasn't us! We swear!" Darlene, though seemingly a seasoned paranormal investigator, acted skeptically toward our explanation. She even scoffed at our excitement over the struck piano key which she suspected was nothing since she didn't hear it herself. I suppose to her mind, we were extremely green investigators who didn't know what we were talking about and who couldn't keep quiet when it was our turn to watch the video feed. An already tentative relationship had become further strained.

Later, through my studies of the paranormal, I would learn that sometimes spirits and the paranormal are sneaky about making noises that only part of a group can hear. For example, only the team members in the kitchen can hear noises in the basement while the rest of the team hears nothing. It could even be only the girls hear the noise while the men are deaf to the sound. Is this a means to separate our team, causing an "us vs. them" mentality? It's entirely possible. Many times, paranormal activity only manifests in the presence of one spouse or one child. For whatever reason, the entity may feel drawn to that one person or, if it's a negative haunting, it could be attempting to separate the family. By separating the family and playing them against one another, the entities—whether they're demonic or just nasty humans who've passed—create a negative energy upon which they can then feed. I believe that is what was happening here. Whatever was in that house could sense that Steve, Stefanie, and I were tense and nervous, and they understood that the cause of our nerves was Darlene who liked to remind us that we were easily replaceable. By not believing us, Darlene simply added fuel to the fire and gave this spirit exactly what it wanted.

As living humans, we like everything to be easy. We like our coffee hot, our beds warm, and life to be uncomplicated. The second we are confronted with something that upsets our neat, orderly reality, such as a spouse or child who is experiencing paranormal activity that we aren't, we tend to scoff. To accept the paranormal is to toss away the easy and uncomplicated. I always tell my clients that they need to give their living loved ones the benefit of the doubt and accept that maybe not everything is as it seems. It may not make our lives easy, but it certainly makes them honest.

Darlene never really did accept the truth of that night and lost a little of our respect in return. That night was the beginning of my realization that the living, like Darlene and myself, didn't have all the answers when it came to the dead.

I AIN'T SKEERED!

I hate the term "ghost hunter." I don't "hunt" anything. I don't have a gun, I don't have traps, I'm not stealthily trying to sneak up on something only to grab it and take it home with me. Well, maybe I sometimes do that with chocolate bars. On the contrary, as Tyler is fond of saying of my avocation, "Just don't bring anything home with you." If you meet someone who calls themselves a ghost hunter, be wary of why they are involved in the paranormal. They are probably out in cemeteries and abandoned buildings for the thrill and not to help people or get answers. True paranormal investigators *work* in this field. We call our clients, write reports, educate the general public, and try to answer the age-old question, "What happens after we die?"

Not only is the term "ghost hunter" annoying, but being compared to *Ghostbusters* is even worse. I can't tell you how many times I hear, "Hey! Have you ever been slimed?!" and I try really hard to just smile rather than throw a copy of *Tobin's Spirit Guide* at them. And even though I don't drive around in a modified ambulance, loaded up with proton packs, I do wish I lived and worked in an old firehouse.

The Gaither Plantation investigation was the first time that I saw all of our equipment being used to its full potential. We were 16 investigators attempting to cover several hundred acres including out-buildings, a large home, a cemetery, and church. We spent the first 90 minutes of the evening setting up infrared cameras, connecting those to a digital video recorder, spreading out various digital voice recorders, and checking everything thoroughly with our electromagnetic field (EMF) meters. It was quite the production, and it was also a chance for me to break out my new EMF meter. I was very proud of it and not only would it give me a digital readout of the EM field in my immediate area—in microTeslas or milliGauss, no less—it would also read the ambient temperature. This is important because a prevailing hypothesis in the paranormal field is that not only will a paranormal entity cause a spike in the EM field when it manifests, it will also cause a drop in the surrounding temperature. This thoughtful birthday gift from Tyler was used to its fullest potential on this night.

But, all the equipment in the world doesn't keep you from being afraid. And I was fearful that night. After Steve, Stefanie, and I migrated through Darlene's blame-game in the house, we were now headed over to the church located on another part of the property. The night had been filled with dark forays into a dank basement full of all sorts of creepy-crawlies, a run-down cemetery where at any moment I was sure to be eaten by a pack of coyotes, and a self-playing baby grand piano. Ironically, I wasn't even concerned with ghosts. Using my voice recorder and EMF meter as shields, I hid my perceived incompetence and fear behind my equipment. I even tried to figure out how to grow a third hand to hold my flashlight. I wanted to impress Darlene, and so far, the night had been a bust in that department.

As Stefanie, Steve, and I shook off the failure of our stint at base camp, the whole team took a quick snack break and attempted to rouse our sleepy minds before we all walked over to the church. It was only two hours before dawn, and we were all yawning and trying unsuccessfully to wake up, but through our sleep deprivation, we hoped this would pan out to be the most active, and interesting, part of our investigation.

Unsubstantiated reports of adultery between a pastor and parishioner, as well as negative paranormal activity, clouded the history of this church. I was tired, hungry, and a little bit over the evening. When the night started, I was gung-ho and ready to do my part. But now, after six hours of investigating, preceded by a long drive, I had the caffeine shakes, and all I wanted was a soft pillow and my Tempur-Pedic bed. As we walked into the sanctuary, I looked longingly at the ache-inducing, joint-stiffening, hard wooden pews and knew I could blissfully slip into unconsciousness with no problem if I were to just lie down on one.

But, that wasn't to be. I took my place in the far end of a pew and turned on my voice recorder and EMF meter. I carefully placed them next to me where they acted as a barrier between me and the rest of the group. While Darlene and the more experienced investigators confidently stood at the front of the church near the baptismal, I made myself small, trying not to get in the way. But, in my extreme fatigue, I was getting punchy. I wanted whatever was there to show itself. It wasn't enough to just record a voice; I wanted to *see* something. I wanted whatever was there to just go ahead and show itself so that I could then get in the backseat of Clint's car and take a two-hour nap. No matter how many times my fellow investigators nicely asked whatever was there to give us some sign of its presence, it wouldn't show itself. I couldn't assume that the shadows I saw in my periphery or the red flashes of light just outside my field of vision were paranormal in nature. I was tired, my eyes were dry, and anything I saw could be chalked up to exhaustion. Fatigue, it seems, was making me brave and reckless.

That very moment I decided to stop being the meek, quiet investigator, and take matters into my own hands. I stood up, abandoned my equipment, and marched down the chapel's center aisle. I shouted, "Show yourself! I'm tired of you taunting us and flitting around the sidelines! I want to see you and I'm over being *played*!"

I'm pretty sure I heard a collective gasp from my fellow investigators. All they had seen of me was the sweet, quiet Heather who observed the others and went along with the crowd. They had never seen this side of me.

I marched around to the rear of the church, hands on my hips, recorder and meter forgotten, ordering the spirits to do my bidding. "Come out! Face me! Let's see what you're made of! Are you cowards? Are you too chicken to show yourself? Why don't you try to knock me down or punch me? I'll bet you're too afraid of me! Well, I'm not afraid of you!"

My team held their breath and waited for my next move. Suddenly, I was running the investigation, not Darlene. I wasn't afraid of what she could do to me or my standing within the team. This wasn't about her, it was about me and my journey. I turned and walked up the center aisle of the church. I looked Darlene in the eye as I said to whatever entities may be listening, "Let's go! If you show yourself to me and my friends, we'll leave. We will get out of your hair. Come on," I cajoled. "Why can't you just show yourself? You can use my energy. You can use the batteries in my equipment. Use that to manifest. Don't you want to prove to us that you're here?"

The rest of my newly-minted investigators followed my lead and began speaking up, daring the spirit to come forward and talk to us. Darlene and her experienced crew at the front of the church could do nothing but watch while I and the rest of my new friends moved to the forefront of the investigation, taking charge. It was a pivotal moment. As Stefanie, Steve, Clint, Jordan, Tammy, and the others took over where I left off, my adrenaline rush faded, and I returned to my corner seat in the pew. Within 30 minutes, Darlene declared the investigation over. We carefully packed our gear in the slowly dawning light and made our way north to our homes in suburban Atlanta. In my sleepy fog, I realized something important about myself. I grasped that I could investigate through and past the fear of rejection and doubt, that no matter how tired, scared, or confused I was, I could own any investigation of which I was a part. And that made me proud.

PARANORBULAR

I t was a dark and stormy night…

No, really. It was early fall and a tropical storm was moving through Atlanta. Already dark and certainly dreary but only slightly stormy, we pulled into the quiet Canton neighborhood, alert to our surroundings and listening to the robotic voice of Clint's GPS guiding us to our client's home. As we pulled into the driveway, we noticed a crowd of umbrellas across the street, shielding a group of neighbors who were watching us pull up to the garage. As we got out of the van, our client rushed across the street to greet us, explaining that she had told her neighbors of our imminent arrival, and that they were there to watch us investigate. We all looked at one another and rolled our eyes. It was to be one of *those* nights.

As we walked through the client's home, hearing her reports of activity and deciding where to place our infrared cameras and EMF meters, the neighbors across the street silently watched us moving back and forth from Clint's van, to the garage, into the house, and back out again. We took the temperature of the living room, trying to determine if the cold spot the client felt while sitting on the couch was an air conditioning vent or something paranormal. I walked throughout the house, using my EMF meter to find those appliances that gave off high EM fields. By doing this, I would know where *not* to place my meter during the investigation. I wanted to find those areas that read zero milliGauss so that if something manifested during the evening, I would know it was paranormal and not, say, the alarm clock going off. While I roamed around, focusing on my meter, the others set up the cameras in the living room, kitchen, and upstairs bedrooms, making sure they were securely screwed onto their tripods, and angled perfectly to film those areas where the client had witnessed fleeting shadows. As we brought the camera cables out into the garage and set up our video recorder and monitor on a folding table, the neighbors across the street observed us through the open garage door.

Finally, the equipment was ready, the cameras were recording, and we were ready to investigate the homeowner's claims of cold spots, darting shadows, and disembodied voices in her 15-year-old, three bedroom, two-and-a-half bath home. We split up into smaller teams and while the first group went inside to conduct the evening's first EVP session, Clint and I took our places in front of the computer screen for the first watch at base camp. Outside, the persistent rain continued to soak the ground as well as the gathered neighbors. The homeowner took pity on them and let them know that if they could stay quiet, they were welcome into the garage. As the curiosity seekers flooded the available space, surrounding Clint, myself, our equipment, and the homeowner's car, the atmosphere became charged. Damp shoes squeaked against the polished concrete and wet umbrellas were hastily collapsed. The smell of steamy clothes and skin permeated the air and immediately, the whispered questions began.

"Where are y'all from?"

"What's the craziest thing you've ever seen?"

"Are there ghosts in there? Did you see anythin'?"

"Tell me, be honest. Are walls drippin' with blood?"

We tried to gamely answer the questions as best as we could. Our normal routine of quiet observance and note-taking had been interrupted, and the inquisitive questions soon became meddlesome. The interrogation came hard and fast and, since I was still fairly new to this paranormal business, I tried to be vague, yet helpful, in my answers. It wasn't easy.

"Well, we're from all around Atlanta. Roswell, Canton, Woodstock, and one of us is from Blue Ridge."

"The craziest thing I've ever seen is dirty diapers laying on a client's kitchen floor, but I don't think that's the answer you want to hear."

"Um, we're not sure if there are ghosts here. That's why we're investigating."

"Really? Blood? Where did you get that?"

Eventually, when the neighbors realized the ghosts weren't going to make an appearance in the garage and we certainly weren't going to allow them to tromp through the house, they began to leave. Whispering amongst themselves, they trickled out into the rain and left us to our own devices.

Except… for that one guy.

I could see him standing behind me, his reflection in the display screen as clear as the black and white infrared picture coming from inside the house. I ignored him, watching the infrared camera feed, making sure the team was fine and that nothing paranormal was happening. Suddenly, the question we had been dreading happened.

"Did y'all just see that orb fly by?!" he suddenly announced.

I turned, looked at him, looked back at the monitor, and rolled my eyes so far back in my head that I swear I could see the underside of my hair follicles. I counted to ten and began my explanation.

"Actually, sir," I said in my most confident mom voice, trying really hard not to use my exasperated mom voice, "that was just dust. Do you see Stefanie there? On the monitor? Well, she just walked by the camera and when she did, it stirred up dust particles on the carpet. When those passed by the camera, they were illuminated by the infrared light on the camera, and what you're seeing are dust particles, not orbs."

"Well," he replied in his thick Southern accent, "I think it was an orb. Them guys on TV said that orbs are ghosts. And that thing was flyin' around pretty good!"

I took a deep, calming breath and counted to ten in my head. "Well, those guys on TV are filming their show for entertainment. Trust me, those are just dust particles. Not ghosts."

He harrumphed at me as he continued to silently watch the camera feeds over my shoulder.

As the investigation carried on through the evening and into the early morning hours, the rain continued to fall and our silent neighbor sentinel stayed with us throughout the investigation, watching the cameras alongside us, asking questions, and being a good sport. When we eventually packed up our equipment, he disappeared into the mist, hopefully better educated on what it is real paranormal investigators do. I like to imagine that when he turned on *Ghost Hunters* a week later, he turned to his wife/child/dog and said, "Did you know that's not a ghost? That's just dust." Since that night, we came up with a new term: paranorbular. It became our secret code word anytime a member of the general public would spout paranormal reality show hypotheses as the gospel truth.

Since becoming an investigator, my fellow team members and I have fielded many questions from clients and the general public about orbs. Pictures are sent to us via email, video clips are submitted through social media, and we've never seen or witnessed a true orb. Let me tell you something right now that I'm going to need for you to repeat to yourself, over and over again, until it becomes second nature. 99.999999999999999999% of "orbs" are dust. The other 0.000000000000000001%? Water droplets, bugs, pollen, and any other particulate matter that may happen to be in the air. For me to accept a photo of an orb as evidence of the paranormal, it would need to be captured in a scientific clean room, an area devoid of dirt, bugs, pollen, moisture, or dust. And if you work in said haunted clean room? Well, good luck, my friend. Dust, rain, pollen, and bugs are easy to catch on film, especially when it's dark. The flash from a camera catches the item that is floating in front of the lens and, suddenly, this minuscule thing is now blurry, large, and overblown in the final picture. Thanks to pareidolia—the human mind responding to an image or a sound by discerning a familiar pattern where none exists—the uneven surface of the dust takes on features. In other words, we interpret those inflated dust particles to be orbs with faces.

It was a little over a year later after our Canton investigation when, out of the blue, I received a Facebook message from a friend I had met through blogging. Mike was going through a very rough time in his life. His son had unexpectedly died, and he was dealing with a lot of depression and anger. I had tried offering words of comfort and support, but I knew those would only be empty words on a screen for him as we lived on opposite sides of the country. That day, though, he sent me a picture. The picture was of Mike, standing in his son's bedroom, surrounded by toy cars, trophies, and childhood memories. In the air around him were orbs.

Mike asked, "Is this my son? Is this him?"

As an experienced paranormal investigator, I knew immediately that, again, I was looking at a photo of illuminated dust particles. As a parent, I knew that he needed to know his son was nearby, surrounding him with love. And so what was my answer? "Yes, Mike. Yes. That is your son. I can see him all around you."

And, technically? Yes, I could. His son was in the swimming ribbon on the shelf, in the Star Wars quilt on the bed, in the stuffed T-Rex resting on the pillow, and especially in Mike's heart and memories. For me, those dust particles were a way of connecting with Mike and giving him comfort. For Mike, those orbs were his son.

Orbs, like ghosts, are all around us. They are the dust covering the souvenirs of our lives. They tend to get stirred up when we pick up a memento or walk by a beloved treasure. They aren't the ghosts we're looking for, but they can certainly remind us of the ghosts we're constantly seeking.

WHY YOU GOTTA
BE LIKE THAT?

I like to jokingly call Tyler's family "The Christmas Mafia." It's not because they overdo it with decorations or cookies or bows or even games. It's because once you attend a Harrell/Dobson family Christmas, you are expected to attend every year thereafter. Some in-laws have legally divorced from the family, but they still come to Christmas every year with their new spouses. It's expected and not at all frowned upon or questioned. His family is just so amazing that if they open their arms and accept you into the fold, well then, deal with it because now you're an official member of the family and good luck getting rid of them! This also extends to the dates of the annual family Christmas celebration. Most of us arrive on December 23rd and leave sometime on the afternoon of the 27th. Tyler's mother will, of course, collapse into a heap immediately thereafter, but don't even think about leaving early because the guilt will be laid on as thick as buttercream icing on a sugar cookie.

I'm telling you all this because one Christmas, I had to leave early on the morning of the 27th. There were many questions as to where I was going and disapproving frowns that I was leaving a few hours early. I left Tyler alone with the kids, kissed all the family goodbye until next year, and headed down the north Georgia mountains in the early morning mist. My sorority sister Toni—the one who helped me track down our college ghost and was witness with me to the chandelier swinging at Rose's funeral—wanted to take her sister to Atlanta's High Museum to see the Chinese terra cotta soldiers from the first emperor's tomb. Not only was this a once-in-a-lifetime opportunity, but I would also get to see friends and gain a little breathing space. Afterward, I would drive to Tucker, Georgia, for a paranormal investigation. It was the perfect end to the Christmas holiday, and even though I felt a twinge of guilt leaving Tyler, the kids, and the rest of the family, I savored the quiet of my car as I directed it south toward Atlanta.

When I arrived at the museum, I immediately saw Toni and her sister, greeting each with hugs and warm words. As we walked into the museum, I was excited to see the exhibit. That is, until I was jostled by the crowd, accosted by several rude museum patrons, and had to battle just for my chance to catch a glimpse of the very exhibit I was there to see. Just two days after Christmas, the time of year when most of America is chanting, "Peace on Earth! Good will toward men!" I realized that said sentiment didn't apply after 12:01 a.m., December 26th, and it certainly didn't apply at fine art museums. I spent most of the morning walking on eggshells, apologizing for every little shoulder bump or need to read a placard. It wasn't a good start to the day, but the terra cotta soldiers were amazing, and I figured that the evening's investigation would more than make up for that day's negativity.

When my team and I arrived at the client's house, we were struck with their youth and their fear of the situation. They couldn't understand what was happening in this, their first home. Not only that, but this home had been the wife's parents' house, passed on to the young couple. They could fix it up, use it as a starter home, and save money for their dream home where they would build their family. The paranormal activity ranged throughout the house and could be felt in each room. The wife felt she was being watched, the husband saw shadows, and they were both very confused and scared. Eventually, when they tore down the old plaster walls to prepare for new drywall, they found a small bundle of animal bones, wrapped in a ribbon, in the wall of the kitchen. That's when they contacted us.

Stefanie and Steve began setting up our cameras throughout the home while Tammy and Clint, our team sensitives, walked through the various rooms. Tammy was a no-nonsense high school teacher, while Clint was a no-nonsense fireman. I looked up to both of them as our group's "Mom and Dad." Even though they had never met each other prior to our group's formation, they worked very well together and both could be counted on to be the voices of reason when the rest of us were acting like inappropriate teenagers. They would independently walk through a home, taking notes as they went, not talking to the client or each other. They never wanted to know about the activity going on and would, therefore, walk in cold. After they were finished, they would compare notes with one another and with the client, and most times, they knew exactly what was happening, where, and why. It was eerie to watch, and I always anticipated what they would say and if it would match our client's claims of the paranormal. This particular night, they both had something disturbing to report.

"I don't like the music room," Clint said, "the room where the husband has all of his guitars."

"Neither do I," Tammy responded. "There's a male spirit in there, and he's angry."

"Bitter," Clint added. "He's not happy about us being here, and he doesn't like the homeowners."

"I think he was an alcoholic when he was alive. And he's very hostile."

For Steve, Stefanie, and I, this news was helpful but also a bit unnerving. We couldn't sense this angry spirit and didn't know if it would lash out at us. As we quietly turned out the lights, invited the homeowners to join us, and slowly moved through the house, we carried our voice recorders ahead of us, nervous of the night to come. And, surprisingly, everything went smoothly until we split up. That's when everything seemed to go wrong.

Tammy and I took up a vigil in the guest bedroom, while Steve and Clint sat in the master bedroom. Across the hall in the music room, Stefanie settled in with the clients. The idea was that we would split up, conduct a wide-ranging EVP session, asking questions, and keeping each other apprised of any personal experiences to see if we could capture better evidence. We found that sometimes, if we only investigated one room at a time, the spirit would escape and hide in another area of the house. By spreading out, we could "get in the spirit's face," so to speak, and not allow it to lie low. But here, in this house, this was a big mistake.

Tammy and I quietly sat on the bed, our voice recorders on the dresser in front of us. We could hear the others quietly talking. Suddenly, from the music room next door, Stefanie cried out. I didn't understand what could have happened as we didn't hear a crash of anything falling or the sound of her tripping, but I knew it sounded like she was in pain. We all rushed to the room and found the homeowners surrounding Stefanie, who was clutching her mid-section.

"We were sitting on the couch," Stefanie exclaimed, "and Mike asked me if I was sensitive like Tammy or Clint. I said no, that I wouldn't know if a spirit walked up to me and went through me. The next thing I knew, I felt something rush up on me and then it felt like I was punched in the stomach!"

I looked over at Clint and then at Tammy, their faces showing shock and surprise. Steve silently shook his head. I knew that my expression mirrored theirs. The clients were nervously leading Stefanie back to the room's couch.

"You know what?" Clint said, "Let's take her out to my van."

Stefanie looked at him with relief, and we all decamped outside, away from whatever had attacked our teammate.

As Stefanie took a long swig from her water bottle, we quietly watched her. Then, she broke the silence.

"That was some fucked up shit," she exclaimed, "and I'm ready to go home."

We all laughed, happy that she seemed fine, and we persuaded her to add a Little Debbie snack cake to her water consumption.

"Well," Clint replied, "let's pack it up!"

As we quickly loaded up our gear, avoiding the music room as much as possible, we calmed the clients, assuring them this wasn't their fault. This was something that we, as investigators, are prepared to deal with. Still, they were shocked and apologetic. Honestly, we were all stunned. This had never happened to any of us on the few investigations we had conducted. For all the supposed pain, scratches, bruises, nausea, headaches, and more that the paranormal reality TV stars suffer, we had escaped our investigations relatively unscathed. Except for the odd trip over a door frame or the annoying errant bug bite, our investigations had been, up to this point, injury-free. Not that night. Two nights after Christmas, I learned a valuable lesson about the dead. They can sometimes be as nasty as the living. My drive home was quiet and introspective, and when I arrived home an hour later, I was grateful to be in my warm, loving home where nothing bitter or angry lurked in the dark, quiet rooms.

Stefanie called me a few days later to tell me that her stomach still hurt and that she had suffered nightmares. This continued for two weeks after the investigation. It was three weeks before the energy from that spiritual punch dissipated and her life returned to normal. I listened carefully to my audio recordings and found that I had captured my very first EVP. Almost one year to the day after joining Atlanta Paranormal Investigations, I discovered a woman's sigh on my voice recorder. While we investigators and the clients had left the house to comfort Stefanie outside, something had leaned in close to my recorder and murmured into its microphone. Was something exasperated with what had happened to our fellow investigator? Was she just over the nonsense perpetrated by the angry man in the next room? I don't know.

I just know that in the midst of Stefanie's fear and pain, something finally decided to talk to me.

When we eventually submitted our final report to the young couple, we let them know that we felt their home definitely had paranormal activity. We encouraged them to contact a member of the clergy to have their home blessed and that we would gladly re-investigate their home, if necessary. We never heard from them again, and I wonder if, much like my day with the rude museum patrons, they spent the rest of their time in their starter home walking on eggshells and trying not to anger the bitter, angry spirit who so spitefully attacked Stefanie.

Many people mistakenly assume that when someone dies, their lingering spirit suddenly transforms to a benign, sweet, innocent ghost that only wants to take care of unfinished business or watch over loved ones. What I've found is that people are in death as they were in life. Bitterness, anger, and malice can exist long after the physical body has been shed. Human spirits can attack, scratch, and be hateful to the living if they are so inclined. They may not be as powerful as inhuman spirits or what Christians commonly refer to as "demons," but they can certainly wreck lives just as effectively.

Eventually, we were able to laugh about that night. Stefanie, understandably, told us that we could count her out if we ever tried to take her back to that small ranch home in Tucker, Georgia.

I'M NOT SAYING IT WAS
ALIENS, BUT IT WAS ALIENS

Typically I'm ready for just about anything when it comes to investigating the paranormal. I've had unexplainable things happen to me that have made my hair stand on end, my heart race, and my voice utter, "What in the heck was that?!" Paranormal things. Ghostly things. But never client things. Not until this one particular investigation. It was that unusual night when Clint, Steve, and I spent five hours in the middle of our very own *X-Files* episode.

As usual, it was a hot, sticky Atlanta summer. My three children were, at the time, aged three, three, and two, and I spent every waking moment chasing after them, cleaning up after them, and trying to generally stay sane. In addition to that, I had just ended a second round of bronchitis and was exhausted from running after my children, coughing, not sleeping, coughing, entertaining my children, coughing… well, you get the idea. The image that sticks most vividly in my brain from that summer is me, in the backyard, fully clothed, slouched in a lawn chair, my feet in the inflatable wading pool, intermittently coughing and sniffling, watching my three children paddle around in the water. We did this every day for three months. I'm sure the sounds of their laughter and squeals, coupled with my hacking, reverberated around our cul-de-sac. By the time our *X-Files* client—let's just call him Fox, shall we?—requested an investigation, my need to get out of the house overrode my need to lay down and bark up a lung. And so, I found myself loaded into the back seat of Steve's pickup truck, coughs muffled in the top of my shirt, trying to convince myself that this was a good idea.

When we pulled up to Fox's home, what I noticed was an older townhome, probably built sometime in the 1980s, brown, with an unkempt yard. We walked up to the front door, Clint knocked, and we waited for Fox to open the door. When he did, I was nearly knocked off my feet. The smell of cigarette smoke hit me first and when I looked down, only to see the burning cigarette he held in between his fingers, I wanted to cry.

"Hello there! Are you the ghost hunters?" he asked. He was a tall, lanky man, hunched over his hand holding the cigarette, white tobacco smoke curling around his head. His black hair, sprinkled with gray, was bushy and unkempt, and his clothes, though clean, hadn't seen the hot face of an iron since they'd been purchased. As is typical for a lifelong bachelor, he wore dark, knee-length socks with his white sneakers.

"Yes!" Clint replied, "We are! My name is Clint, this is Steve, and this is Heather."

Fox reached out to shake each of our hands in turn and welcomed us into his home. The first thing I noticed about Fox, besides his smoking habit, was that he was staunch defender of the rights of dust mites, because the layer of grime on every piece of furniture was impressive. Even more impressive was the yellow nicotine tinge every surface seemed to carry.

"Well," Fox said, "I'm sure you all know what's going on here."

"We do, we do," Clint replied, "We've all read your phone interview transcript and gone over the reports of activity, but you are welcome to show us around and give us a summary of what's going on where so that we know where to put our equipment and investigate."

As Fox showed us through the living room and then back to the dining room and kitchen, he recounted his time in the military. As a retired Army colonel, he claimed to be privy to many top secret documents and occurrences. I quietly figured that after decades living in the military, his current unkempt appearance and living space was a quiet sort of mutiny. As we continued walking through his house, I tried very hard to hold back the coughs building in my chest. My bronchitis had, I thought, finally taken a back seat, but it seemed that my mucus sensed the smoke party going on in Fox's house and wanted to join in the fun. Once in the small kitchen, Fox began recounting his experiences.

"Now, I will stand back here, at the sink, and look out my window while I wash dishes. Do you see the woods back there?"

We three peeked over Fox's shoulder, avoiding the pile of dirty dishes piled in the sink, and looked into the gloomy stand of trees between his house and the nearby highway.

"That's where the aliens land."

My need to cough was suddenly overridden by my need to shove my eyebrows up into my hairline. Aliens? I mean, I knew by reading the report on this client that he felt there were aliens involved, but to actually hear him say it was another thing entirely.

"I've always known they existed," he told us conspiratorially, waving his cigarette dangerously close to our faces, "because I've seen the documents. I know for a fact the government is trying to cover up the truth that they're here on Earth. And now, they're here in my neighborhood. I think it's because I know too much."

I didn't have a mirror in front of me, but I'm pretty sure my eyes were as big as flying saucers and my mouth was open in surprise. Or, I could have been gasping for air, about to pass out from the lack of oxygen. Either scenario was possible.

My thoughts were broken by a kitchen timer going off, and it was then I noticed, underneath the malodor of smoke and nicotine, the odor of something cooking. And it wasn't at all pleasant. Fox excitedly put on hot mitts, opened the oven, and took out a cookie sheet full of... not cookies. All I could see was bacon, which was promising, wrapped around little brown lumps of something.

"I made these for you guys!" Fox exclaimed, "They're my favorite hors d'oeuvres, and I thought you all might enjoy them too! Here, try some!"

And as I opened my mouth to protest, to tell him, "Thanks, but no thanks, I just had dinner," he popped one of those horrid morsels in my mouth. I immediately shut my mouth and held the food there, not chewing.

"It's liver paté wrapped in bacon! My specialty! What do you think?"

I began chewing because to gag, spit it out, wipe my tongue on his dish towel, and run out his front door would have been seen as impolite. Any and all negative childhood memories involving liver were dredged up to the forefront of my mind, and I was immediately reminded why I hated this particular cut of the cow. It seemed that instead of receiving an alien anal probe, I was to endure a paté probe. But, proper manners dictate politeness and courtesy, so, instead of booking it out the front door, I said, "Great! That's awesome! Thanks!" and asked to be excused to the bathroom where I coughed, gagged, spit, made several awful faces, and washed my mouth out with tap water. Clint and Steve looked horrified, not because I nearly choked, but because they were the next victims in this liver paté-bacon-alien mouth probe debacle.

Once I returned, Fox picked up where he left off and launched into his experiences over the last twenty years. As a recently retired US Air Force colonel with that aforementioned top secret clearance, he was convinced that aliens were not only landing on his property, but also abducting his neighbors, replacing them with clones, and spying on him from inside his home. He showed us a crack in the ceiling over his bed where he was sure the aliens had placed a camera to watch him. He took us upstairs to the spare bedroom and showed us the dusty shelf where he had found a small, handprint in the grime and even showed us the picture he had taken of said handprint. It was small and consisted of just three fingers. It looked like E.T. had walked out of the closet, grabbed hold of the shelf for support, and then walked away. Could Fox have created the handprint himself and "rediscovered" it a few days later? It was entirely possible and the most plausible explanation. In Fox's mind, though, that three-fingered handprint looked alien, and it fit his narrative. In the end, though, I could neither explain the strange print's presence nor how it was made.

I had managed, by now, to calm my cough, and Fox asked if, before we set up our equipment, we could go outside to see the aliens' landing site. We obliged and gamely walked out, waiting for him on the front porch. It was a clear, albeit humid, evening, and we turned on our flashlights so that we could safely make our way through the overgrown brush and trees. As Fox tripped over a log, out of his pocket fell a 9mm Glock handgun. My life passed before my eyes, because I somehow knew that that gun wasn't for show. It was most likely fully loaded. Fox stumbled around, picked up the gun, and muttered, "Can't see where I'm going. I don't trust these replacements to not try to stop us from being out here, that's why I brought my gun. Can't be too careful."

"Replacements?" I asked.

"Most of these people," he gestured with his gun-free hand, "have been abducted by the aliens, taken away for experiments, and replaced with people who look like them but aren't them."

Steve, Clint, and I were silent. None of us knew how to respond to such a claim. I kept staring at the gun, thanking providence for not allowing it to go off when it hit the ground. As Fox continued to talk, he put the gun back in his shorts pocket.

"It's mostly been the women who have been replaced. But a few of the men too. This house right here," he gestured to his next door neighbor, "and that house over there," he pointed to a house two doors down, "were the first to go."

Just then, a car drove into a driveway across the street. The gentleman got out, saw us, and waved. "Hey, Fox! How's it going?"

"Good!" Fox shouted back. "Real good! Work okay?"

The neighbor walked toward his door and hollered back, "Just fine! Keeping us busy! Have a good night!" and walked into his house.

Fox was quiet for a moment and then said, "That's not him. He's been replaced too."

Clint, Steve, and I stared at one another with wide eyes. Prior to meeting Fox, we wondered if maybe we could be dealing with a delusion rather than actual aliens. Now, we knew for sure that was the case.

"Well," Clint said, "I think we'll set up our equipment now."

Back inside the smoke-filled, nicotine-coated home, my lungs again began to protest. The brief respite of fresh air was something they didn't want to give up, and they rejected the fetid air in protest. Thankfully, for me and my lungs, Fox took up vigil outside on his porch and allowed Clint, Steve, and I to investigate alone and unencumbered. The first thing I did was check his medicine cabinet because I wanted to make sure we weren't dealing with someone taking drugs for a mental condition. All I could find was aspirin and antacid, which actually wasn't a relief. A pharmaceutical explanation for our client's behavior would have been better than the reality of his situation. Finally, we began our investigation in earnest.

The kitchen suffered from a very high electromagnetic field which was understandable. The appliances were as old as the house and not well-shielded. Given the small size of the kitchen and the close proximity of said older appliances, the entire area was awash in a higher-than-normal EM field. If Fox was physically susceptible to high EM fields, he could be experiencing any number of side effects, including paranoia, which made perfect sense considering that he claimed to see figures of aliens in the trees from his kitchen window.

But nowhere else in the house did the EM field rise above a zero milli-Gauss reading. We were perplexed and began our first EVP session in the upstairs bedroom where Fox had spotted the three-fingered handprint. Fox lived on the main floor of his small townhome and used the upstairs as storage for the detritus of his life. Though the downstairs was neat, it was most definitely a bachelor pad, with mismatched furniture, dusty plants, and a floor that desperately needed to be introduced to a vacuum. The upstairs, though, had been mistreated. It was the red-headed stepchild of Fox's home. Rather than taking the opportunity to have a spare bedroom and adjoining office, he had left those rooms empty and, quite literally, tossed the half-forgotten memories of his life across the floor. We tried to find open space on the carpet amidst the scattered books, lamps, and discarded clothing. When we finally settled in, I stared across the room to the open doorway that led to the hall. My coughing slowly, but surely, increased in frequency, and I was now constantly fighting a losing battle and sipping water, hoping to quell it. As I quietly sat and listened to Clint and Steve ask whatever was there to show itself, I saw what looked like a shadow come between Steve and I, hands raised.

"Steve!" I exclaimed. "Did you just move?"

"No," he replied. "I didn't budge."

"You sure?" I asked. "You didn't raise your hands to stretch or anything?"

"Nope," he said. "My hands have been on my legs this whole time."

I couldn't explain that shadow and none of us could rationalize the noises coming from the room's closet. Each time we heard a shuffling or scraping, we would open the door only to see…nothing. I had battled a family of raccoons in my attic a few years back, and I knew what they sounded like inside the walls of a home. We also had flying squirrels at the time. A whole danged Georgia critter menagerie had taken up residence in the rafters of our attic. In this case, though, we weren't hearing animals in the walls. This was a scraping on the door itself. But there was nothing there.

Finally, after three hours of wandering through Fox's home, sitting in the dark, and fighting against the rising tightness in my chest, I looked at Clint and Steve and said, "I'm done. I can't breathe, and I feel like there's an elephant on my chest. I just need to get out of here." The guys, to their credit, said not a word. They turned on the lights and started disassembling cameras while I went outside to gulp in lungfuls of air that hadn't been tainted by decades of lit Marlboros. We thanked Fox for his kind hospitality, agreed that his bacon-wrapped liver paté was certainly… something, and told him that we would review our evidence and send him our final report as soon as possible. We all loaded into Steve's truck and drove away. I collapsed in the back seat and as soon as we turned out of Fox's neighborhood, we all started laughing. We weren't making fun of Fox. Instead, it was a release. Fox's insistence about the aliens abducting his neighbors, his need to carry—and carelessly handle—a firearm in our presence, and my illness made it the most surreal night any of us had ever had. As our laughter died down, I devolved into a coughing fit.

In the ensuing days, as I recovered from smoke inhalation and accidental liver consumption, I went over and over Fox's situation. Was he truly being visited by extra-terrestrials? Was he suffering from a mental illness or the beginnings of dementia? Did his years in the Air Force contribute to an already-present paranoia that was now dangerously out of control? I have no idea. It was clear that this gentleman, an intelligent, retired military officer, was absolutely convinced he was in the middle of, and a subject of, a secret alien genetic collection field trip. After going over all of our audio and video footage, we had nothing to report. The noises from the closet weren't picked up on audio and the infrared camera didn't record the shadow I had seen with my own eyes. All we had to show for the night was a smattering of personal experiences and a vow to never again investigate the home of a heavy smoker. My intuition told me that there was nothing supernatural, paranormal, or extraterrestrial going on inside Fox's townhome or throughout his neighborhood. My gut firmly believed that unchecked delusion was the culprit, and the only cure for that was therapy and pharmaceuticals.

And did we help him? Honestly, I don't think we were of any comfort whatsoever. Whether we believed him or not, whether we believed in E.T.s or UFOs or not, we couldn't just discount him based on his beliefs versus ours. Regardless of any of that, what he was feeling was valid. The events he described to us might not have actually happened, but his sleep-deprived eyes, his loaded firearm, and his paranoia were truly happening.

And that worries me to this day.

SHOPPING
WITH SHADOWS

I magine standing in your local Bath and Body Works and feeling a tap on your shoulder as you take a sniff of the rose-scented lotion in your hand. As you turn to see who is attempting to grab your attention, you realize you're the only customer in the store and the manager is behind the counter, ten feet away. Or how about standing in the dressing room at Macy's and hearing someone giggle as you attempt to try on the designer jeans two sizes too small for you? Except, there's no one in there with you. Maybe you're salivating over the latest purple leather Coach purse and catch a whiff of cigar smoke, except there are no smokers walking or loitering nearby. What if your day of retail therapy was touched by the paranormal? It was for this very reason that we found ourselves at a local Atlanta-area mall that had reports of ghostly activity.

Shopping malls take on a whole different feel at night. During the day, they're bustling with the cacophony of hundreds of voices and delicious smells—Auntie Anne's Pretzels, right? At night, they are dark and eerily quiet, and any noise immediately echoes off the cavernous structure. When it first opened, this particular mall in the North Atlanta suburbs had five anchor stores. Eventually, one of those stores closed and the space became a storage area for the mall's holiday decorations.

Since the store's closing, security guards and mall employees reported seeing shadows and hearing voices within the now-defunct store. It became such a distraction to all the employees that mall management had allowed the security guards to call us to investigate.

When we first arrived, Tom, the security guard who asked us to investigate, led us back to the electrical room where gigantic breaker switches controlled the store's electricity.

"I figured you guys could set up your computer equipment in here," he said, "and make this your home base."

Immediately, I felt the hair on my neck and arms stand straight up, and my head felt tingly. I grabbed my EMF meter and turned it on. The electromagnetic field was so high that the meter's screen just showed dashes. I was surfing the wave of an EM buzz.

"You guys," I said, "check out your meters. This place is hoppin'!"

Everyone gathered around, and we moved as one throughout the room, waiting for the meter to change. It didn't, at least not until we walked out of the electrical room and several feet down the hall.

"Wow," Jordan exclaimed, "that's nuts. Tom, we can turn those breakers off during the investigation, right?"

"Oh, yeah," he replied, "definitely!"

We continued down the back hallway and returned to the store. Now devoid of clothes and appliances, it was a large, cavernous space interspersed with Christmas flowers, Santa's chair, giant Easter eggs, the Easter Bunny's enormous basket, and unused kiosks. There were two floors connected by an escalator that hadn't been turned on in several years. As we walked around, taking our electromagnetic field readings, making sure nothing else was giving off a high EM field, Tom filled us in on the history of the mall and his experiences when the crowds went home.

"You know," he began, "a lot of people say there was a murder here."

"Really?" Stefanie asked.

"Yep," he replied. "Back before they built this mall, this was all a large, wooded area. A couple of houses here and there, but not much. It was pretty empty. Supposedly, a boy was murdered somewhere around here."

"Wow," Clint replied. "That could certainly fuel any paranormal activity that may be going on here. What kind of things are you experiencing?"

"Well," Tom scratched his chin, "we see a lot of shadows and hear footsteps. And it's not just here in this old store. A few of the other stores close by will experience things. I think the manager in the Yankee Candle got tapped on the shoulder and she hadn't even opened the store yet!"

"Yeah, I'd quit that job pretty quick," I muttered.

"Now, this hasn't happened, here," he continued, "but a few of the other stores report merchandise being moved or broken during the night when they're closed. Of course, you guys can't investigate those places because of the different policies of the franchises."

"I tried calling a few of the managers," Clint said, "but none could allow us to come in. Kind of disappointing."

"Well," Tom sighed, "I think there'll be enough activity here that you'll be pretty busy for the night."

We all nodded our heads and began breaking off to our assignments. While Stefanie and I took baselines of the entire space, Clint and Jordan began setting up cameras. Tammy walked through on her own, attempting to get a feeling for the location and what may be there waiting for us. Finally, we finished setting up our infrared cameras and decided to stick together in one large group of five. Tom then turned off the lights. Suddenly, the cheery Christmas poinsettias and giant pastel spring flowers took on menacing proportions, and I honestly began to wonder if the mall Easter Bunny would jump out at us from the abandoned kiosks. Except he would have bloody fangs. I really hate the Easter Bunny.

As Clint, Jordan, Stefanie, Tammy, and I took to the escalator to walk down to the first floor, our footsteps loudly echoed across the still, metal steps. In the distance, we could hear the janitorial service polishing the floors of the mall. Light from the parking lot filtered down the escalator and we slowly made our way around the first floor. We began asking our standard questions, hoping something would answer.

"What is your name?" Jordan asked.

A half-minute later, Tammy added, "How did you die?"

After another lengthy pause, giving whatever spirit was there time to answer, Clint asked, "Why are you here?"

Eventually, as we moved from housewares to bedding, the questions transitioned from general to specific.

"Were you murdered on this property?" Stefanie inquired.

"How were you murdered?" I added.

Gradually, the questions tapered off and the inevitable happened.

"So, Heather, how are the kids?" Tammy asked.

"Again with the kids?!" Jordan exclaimed, exasperated.

I snorted with laughter.

Even though our EVP sessions always began with good intentions—trying to talk to the spirits that may be in our presence—we would ultimately move on to casual conversation about our lives. Slowly, the gossip faded, and we found ourselves back where we had started at the bottom of the escalator. We had investigated for a full hour with no results, and we decided to change tactics. The only part of the first floor we hadn't investigated was the old children's department. It was across from the bottom of the escalator, devoid of holiday decorations, and completely dark. Unlike the rest of the first floor, the children's department was farthest from the mall entrance and completely lacking any windows or lights from outside. We decided it was time to give the spirits the silent treatment and quietly sit down for a spell. We gathered around a column, settled in, and rested our tired bones, equipment still recording and noting any changes in the EM field and temperature.

As I scanned the first floor from my vantage point, thanks to the light filtering in from above, my eyes could make out the bottom of the escalator. I silently despaired that my stomach and intestines would never shut up and was just trying really hard not to belch, fart, sneeze, cough, or sniff. Honestly? That's pretty much always going through my mind on an investigation. I intently watched the foot of the escalator and scanned back and forth, observing and waiting.

Out of nowhere, I saw a man pass in front of the escalator. Well, not a man, exactly. It was a tall, black shadow. At least six feet tall, I could clearly see the head, shoulders, arms, and upper torso. But past that, there was nothing. What I could see was black. There were no features, no face or hair, just a seamless black shadow. One moment it wasn't there, the next it was. It silently walked, or glided, from left to right, in front of the escalator and then disappeared. There was no sound, and I knew immediately that whatever it was, it wasn't a living human being. My breath caught in my throat as I dealt with what I just saw. It took a moment for my brain to process the shadow without a body and, a few seconds later, when I finally accepted that I had just seen a ghost, I whispered, "Did you guys just see that?!"

Tammy, who was sitting to my right and was also staring at the escalator, replied, "I wondered when you were going to say something!"

"There... there... guys! It was a shadow! Just now!" I sputtered.

"Yep!" Tammy grinned.

"No way!" Jordan responded. "Where?"

I got up, walked over to the foot of the escalator, and demonstrated what I saw, "There was a shadow! Right here! And it walked just like this and was absolutely quiet!"

Stefanie took out the walkie-talkie and radioed to Tom who was still upstairs in the electrical room. She verified that neither he nor anyone on his staff had walked down the escalator. Nope, we were the only ones down here.

Clint and I frantically began searching the first floor, making absolutely certain that another guard on Tom's staff hadn't inadvertently come downstairs, not knowing we were investigating. But, after an exhaustive search, and finding no extra humans in the area, we had only one conclusion.

Tammy and I had just spotted an honest-to-goodness ghost.

Tom ran downstairs to join us, and we repeated the story, showing him what we had witnessed.

"Really? That's what you saw? Wow, I see that practically every night!"

We all stared at him, mouths agape.

"Lucky duck," I whispered.

After everyone calmed down and Tom headed upstairs, we tried once again to entice whatever was there to come out and show itself a second time. We quietly sat back down in the children's department, silently watching the escalator, and waited.

And waited.

And waited.

The mall spirit refused to show itself again that night. Making sure the mall was secure from thieves and vandals was a difficult enough job for Tom, but trying to keep his employees from quitting over ghostly shenanigans was enough to make his head spin. Knowing a group of people had just validated his experiences and didn't run away screaming made him a very happy man.

Whenever someone asks me, "What was the scariest thing that ever happened to you?" I recount this investigation each and every time. It was my first shadow, my first unexplainable experience, my first "What the…?" moment. But it wasn't at all scary. On the contrary, it was exhilarating!

THE REALITY OF
HUNTING GHOSTS

When watching reality ghost hunting TV shows, there is a big disparity between what they do and what paranormal investigators like me do. First of all, the investigators on the TV shows have a production crew that has secured, and paid for, the use of an historic location. The stars of the show will go to said location for several nights, having full run of the place. They will have their travel scheduled and paid for by the production company, hotel rooms reserved, and a craft service to feed them. All they have to do is get plenty of sleep, show up, and investigate.

When we investigate a location, it's almost always a private home that we have been asked to investigate. The home or business owners aren't always the easiest people to get along with, plus we have to battle time off from jobs and family responsibilities, fight horrific Atlanta traffic, and dance around the threat of intestinal distress from bad gas station food. Through all of that, we're lucky if we have the location to ourselves for four, maybe five, hours. The grand historical buildings the TV show ghost hunters investigate are most always clean and neat. Otherwise, their production crew provides them with face masks. We never know what kind of environments we're going to find. Sometimes, the house is clean and beautiful. Other times, there may be dried, sticky soda coating the kitchen floor and trash strewn across the living room. Sometimes, our clients are a psychologist's dream.

It's not a glamorous job. Heck, it's not even a job. The reality show investigators receive a salary, per diem, travel allowance, and probably even a clothing allowance to do what they do. We get paid... nothing. Everything we do is on a volunteer basis because it's frowned upon in the paranormal community to charge for our services. Sure, we've had clients fix us food—not counting that horrific bacon-wrapped liver paté debacle. We've even had clients make small monetary donations that we use toward new equipment or gasoline, but getting paid a salary for this is something that's never happened. Lastly, when the investigation is all over, even if we've done the leg work, discovered what's going on in the client's home and why, there are no accolades, no press tours, no swag bags, no crowds to cheer us on and ask for our autographs. There is only the possibility that we'll someday find that one piece of evidence that will prove, irrevocably, that ghosts exist.

When Anne came to Atlanta Paranormal's monthly meeting, I was a bit confused. We'd never had a client join us for a meeting, but Darlene insisted that they were friends and that Anne had a story we needed to hear. After we finished our waffles, bacon, and coffee, we migrated to the upstairs of the Roswell J. Christopher's / Public House. As we settled in, we could hear the restaurant patrons below. The scraping of forks and knives against plates was muffled, but the sweet smell of syrup wafted up to our noses. Even though I was full, the smells were still enticing. Darlene's involvement with the group had tapered off, and she left the work to the rest of us. This was the first meeting she had attended in months and even though we were annoyed by her presence, we accepted it and got to work. Over the previous two years, this site of my first investigation had become a welcoming home, a place I dwelled in each month with my fellow investigators for meetings. I still imagined Michael and Catherine, the ghostly Civil War star-crossed lovers, watching us from the shadowy corners, giving us their blessing. But, on this day, visions of the ghostly couple faded as Anne began to tell us her story.

"My house is haunted," she began, standing at the front of the room, "and I need your help."

Of course, this was something we'd heard before, but we still listened intently to her account.

"I'm hearing a lot of voices and seeing shadows and… I just don't know what to do. I'm scared. My children are in college, I just recently got a divorce, and I hate being alone in that house."

She truly sounded frightened, and as we began to ask questions, taking notes on what she was saying, Tammy and Clint, who had been whispering to each other in the back, interrupted her.

"Hey, guys," Tammy declared. "There's something negative here."

We all froze. Tammy didn't make such claims lightly, and if she said there was something negative in the room, she was telling the truth.

"Yeah," Clint responded. "It's like a black shadow standing in the front of the room, watching us."

We all scanned the front of the room, trying to make out whatever it was that could be there with us. I couldn't see or sense anything, but that didn't mean the negative presence wasn't there. Anne, meanwhile, had frozen in place at the front of the room, a look of terror in her eyes. She slowly moved over to a table, sat down, and continued her story.

"I would really appreciate it if you guys could come out to my house. Darlene and I have been friends for years, and she assures me that you all can help me get rid of whatever is there," Anne stated.

We all excitedly agreed that, yes, we would help, but Tammy added, "We don't cleanse houses or get rid of spirits. Our job is to simply investigate and validate activity. What you do with your home and the spirits after we leave is up to you. We can recommend a member of the clergy for a blessing, but that's as far as we go."

"I understand," Anne replied. "I just need someone to tell me I'm not crazy."

As the meeting broke up, we set a date and time for Anne's investigation and I drove home, mulling over the negative presence at our meeting, wondering if it was a transient spirit or if it had taken up permanent residence at the Public House. I worried that Catherine and Michael may have unpleasant company in their ghostly home.

When we arrived at Anne's house two weeks later, we found ourselves in the heart of Roswell, Georgia, in a nice suburban neighborhood. The house, constructed in the mid-1990s, was a typical Atlanta home of the period. Stucco covered the front of the house while siding surrounded the remaining three sides, and it resided in a quiet upper-middle-class cul-de-sac. Basically, there was nothing special about Anne's house from the outside. It was what was going on inside that had our full attention.

That night, I had decided to forgo my usual uniform of jeans and team shirt because it was late-June and extraordinarily humid. But, with my recent weight-loss, none of my shorts fit. I had just discovered the wonder of... skorts! Don't judge. As a mom with less-than-desirable bulges and folds, fixable only through plastic surgery and several hours of spin class each week, I use any means necessary to hide the cellulite, and skorts, not diamonds, are a mom's best friend. And so, I found myself at Anne's house in my black team shirt, our logo proudly emblazoned across my back, paired with a brand new cream-colored skort.

Steve, Clint, and Jordan, being guys, couldn't help but give me a hard time about wearing a skirt on an investigation and reminded me, "How are you going to run in that thing if a ghost jumps out and scares you?"

Stefanie and Tammy, meanwhile, applauded my fashion sense and said I looked cute.

We finally settled down to the investigation, and Clint, Jordan, and I started off in the kitchen. Anne had left us to our own devices, going out to dinner at a nearby restaurant. The lights from the various appliances lit up the space, and we found we had no need for our flashlights. We began asking our general questions, moving into more specific questions about Anne and her family.

Suddenly, Jordan exclaimed, "Did you hear that?"

Instantly, we were energized.

"What was it?" I asked.

"It was a male voice, to my left, and it said something." he replied.

"What did it say?" Clint asked.

Jordan responded, "I'm not sure. I just know it was a man's voice. I'll mark the time and check my recorder later to see if I captured it on audio."

We continued our session, eventually moving upstairs to Anne's bedroom, where she had experienced a great deal of activity. I knew that Anne had cats, seeing them earlier before she shut them up in the basement. As we settled into various spots in her bedroom, I could smell what I thought was the litter box. As a cat-owner myself, I knew the ammonia-laden smell of cat urine, and I suspected the litter box was nearby in her bathroom. I sat down on the floor at the foot of Anne's bed while Clint and Jordan settled in a chair and on the bed, respectively.

We began our EVP session, and I began to regret my lower position in the room. The smell of cat urine was strong and getting stronger by the minute. I silently listened to Jordan ask questions, trying unsuccessfully to mask my nose with my hand. Gradually, I realized that my backside was damp. It took a moment for my brain to register what was happening, and when it did, I jumped up off the floor and exclaimed, "I've been sitting in *cat pee!*"

Jordan and Clint immediately burst out laughing. I danced around the end of the bed, feeling my bum, kneeling down on the carpet and closely sniffing the spot where I sat. Sure enough, the carpet was damp and reeked of feline urine.

"Dammit! I can't believe I sat in cat pee! And this skort is brand new!" I shouted.

Jordan and Clint were doubled over in laughter, barely able to talk. I disgustedly shook my head and marched over to the foot of the chair where Clint sat. I carefully felt the carpet and muttered, "I'll bet the all-famous Ghost Hunters never investigate places where there's cat pee on the carpet."

Jordan snorted, and we all quieted back down, ready to get back to the business at hand. Unfortunately, the mood had been broken, and we only remained in the bedroom for a few more minutes before rejoining the rest of the team downstairs. Anne had returned from dinner, and she was ready to investigate her own home along with us. We all trooped back upstairs, returning to her bedroom, with our full investigative complement, and took up stations throughout the bedroom, bathroom, and closet. Steve and I looked around the darkened closet, the garage directly underneath us. Before lowering myself to the carpet, I patted it and leaned down on all fours to take a sniff. When I looked up, dresses and blouses brushing my shoulders, Steve was giving me a funny look.

"What the heck, Heather?" he asked.

"Um, nothing." I muttered. "It's all good."

Thankfully, the carpet was dry. Anne sat in the bedroom, and she began the EVP session.

"Why are you here?!" she aggressively asked.

We all looked at one other, surprised at her combative tone. Except for my out-of-character outburst at Gaither Plantation, caused by a lack of sleep and coffee, we tried to make it a habit to never provoke the spirits we investigated. But, if the client wanted to do it, we certainly wouldn't stop them.

"You need to leave me alone and leave my house! I don't want you here!" Anne shouted.

"Can you tell us if you have a message for Anne?" Tammy benignly asked.

"Maybe I don't want your message," Anne retorted.

"Well," I said loudly to be sure they heard me from the closet, "I would like to know what your message is. Why don't you tell me?"

This back and forth went on for several more minutes, Anne determined to confront whatever was there while we interjected with more calm questions.

Suddenly, as if in response to her angry questions, we heard a loud crash from below. It sounded as if every shelf in Anne's garage had been knocked over in one swoop. Steve and I looked at each other, mouths gaping. Our equipment was down there. Without thinking, the two of us jumped up and ran out of the closet, down the hall, and practically flew down the stairs. The rest of the team, confused, started shouting, "Hey! What's wrong?! *Where* are you *going?!*"

The heat of the summer night had prompted us to leave Anne's garage doors open which made us wonder if someone had snuck in and tried to steal our equipment, knocking it over in the process.

Panting, we skidded to a stop in the garage, wildly looking around, Steve for an intruder to yell at and punch, me for a ghost to try to document and capture. We were both disappointed. The garage was devoid of anyone, living or dead, and everything was as we had left it 30 minutes before. Outside, the crickets chirped, cars passed on the distant highway, and our digital video recording system silently documented the footage of our infrared cameras. Whatever noise we heard, it wasn't caused by anything being knocked over or thrown around. Jordan, Stefanie, Tammy, Clint, and Anne followed close behind, and while Anne checked out her garage for anything that may be out of place, we investigators looked at each other and began frantically whispering.

"Why did you run down here so fast?" Clint asked, exasperated.

"I wasn't going to let some idiot get away with stealing our equipment!" Steve exclaimed.

"Holy crap, Clint! That was loud! Steve and I could feel it in the closet! I wanted to see if things were getting thrown off the shelves due to poltergeist activity!" I emphatically stated.

"Well, don't run off like that again without the rest of the team!" Clint said, "Someone could have been in here and could have hurt you two when you rushed out like that!"

Jordan shook his head and looked around the garage, "What the heck was that you guys? I mean, nothing is moved!"

"I know," I responded. "I don't get it either."

"This place is just nuts." Tammy flatly responded. We all agreed.

Anne walked back over and stated that nothing was out of place. It wasn't like any other experience she had ever had before. We returned inside, only this time to the living room. There, we set up a Frank's Box, a radio that is set to continuously scan the AM frequency band, creating a sort of white noise generator that the spirits can possibly manipulate and speak through. Imagine an Ouija board that talks back to you, and that's what a Frank's Box is. It's a very experimental piece of equipment and not one we typically use with a client present. This time, though, Anne insisted on being with us. Stefanie turned on the Frank's Box radio and began asking the standard EVP questions, which resulted in... nothing. Soon, though, Anne became frustrated and began asking her own questions. Again, her questions were aggressive, and I could feel the atmosphere in the room changing, becoming heavy. Suddenly, the Frank's Box began responding with words you would never hear spoken on the AM band.

"Bitch!"

"Whore!"

The words were uttered in a strong, guttural male voice. And those were just two of the words spit out at us. I won't put the others here because of their horrible nature, but suffice it to say that Stefanie immediately turned the Frank's Box off, and we told Anne that we could no longer conduct the session with the Box because of the negativity coming through it.

After that, we decided it would be best to end the investigation for the night. As we gradually took the infrared cameras off tripods and wrapped up the numerous cables, I overheard Clint talking to Tammy in the living room, their low tones keeping their conversation quiet enough not to be heard by Anne in the kitchen, but as I passed by, I paused and listened in.

"You remember when she came to our meeting? And you and I sensed a negative spirit at the restaurant?" Clint asked.

"Yeah! I was just thinking about that!" Tammy replied. "That spirit wasn't attached to the restaurant. It's attached to Anne."

"Exactly!" Clint exclaimed, "I saw it here, again, tonight, when Anne was investigating with us!"

"That negativity is hers," Tammy stated.

I walked away and continued to wrap my cable. We eventually loaded up our cars and left. All the way home, I smelled cat pee and thought about what Clint and Tammy had said. We weren't sure of what had brought the negative energy into Anne's home, but unfortunately, it was there to stay unless she did something about it. When we turned in our final report to Darlene, she was very dismissive of our findings from the night. She forwarded the report to Anne and didn't seem all that worried that her friend was sharing living space with something or someone that wanted to cause chaos in her life.

I don't know what ever became of Anne and her negative spirit. But, I do know that I finally washed the cat pee out of my skort—with a mix of OxyClean and detergent using hot water through not just one, but two loads—and never again wore it on an investigation.

MOM'S HOUSE

"Dammit, Heather! I just hate these damned Georgia cockroaches!" Mom grumbled.

"Well, you're the crazy fool who moved down here!" I saucily replied.

"Ungrateful brat," she muttered back.

My mother's hate-hate relationship with the gigantic Georgia cockroach is legendary in our family. She will call the local exterminator, who will gamely come out to her house and sprinkle death dust around her attic and house perimeter. Then, she'll gleefully call me over the next week, describing in full detail the wholesale slaughter of those roaches who dared enter her sanctuary. Everything will quiet down for a few days until I receive the inevitable 6 a.m. follow-up phone call that typically goes something like this:

"Sonuva... I had to get up in the middle of the night to pee, and I'll be damned if there wasn't a roach on the wall right above the toilet paper," she said between, I'm sure, gritted teeth. "I knocked it off with a magazine and hit it so hard it left a mark. I hate those damned things!"

Since her permanent move from West Virginia to Georgia in July, 2005, I've told Mom time and again that to declare war on the Georgia cockroaches is a futile thing. It's hot and humid 11 months out of the year. January is chilly and then flowers start sprouting in February. Which means we get three, maybe four, weeks tops that are cockroach free. Of course, I'm a native West Virginian which means I'm probably exaggerating about the weather and the bug situation down here. But that's only because bugs and heat are gross.

One evening, after Tyler and I had put the kids to bed and crashed on the couch with Netflix and chocolate, I received what I thought was yet another bug-related phone call. It wasn't that at all.

"Heather. The vent fan over the stove just came on!" she said, exasperated.

I was a bit skeptical. "By itself?"

"*Yes*, by itself!" she practically shouted, "And I can't get it to turn off! What do I do?"

"Um, how about you turn the breaker off and back on? Maybe that will do it," I helpfully replied.

And that worked. It was odd, but hey, houses can be screwy, so we just waited to see if it would happen again.

It didn't. But something else did.

"Heather," she asked over the phone a few days later, as I was washing dishes and trying to keep the kids from killing one another, "did you come over to my house this week?"

"Um, no," I replied. "Why?"

"Well, I went into my upstairs guest bathroom to get some toilet paper and something was moved," she replied.

"Okay. Are you sure it's something you may have moved and forgot about?" I asked.

"Good Lord, Heather, I'm old, but I'm not addled," she huffed. "You know those foam flowers I have on the back of the toilet in there?"

"Yep!" I replied, concentrating on her question while my eyes focused on Jarrod with a death stare sure to stop him from stealing Heath's toy. "Sure do!"

"Well," she said, "One of those flowers is now hanging on the shower head."

"What the heck?" I exclaimed.

"I know!" she cried. "I can't figure it out! I would never put one on the shower head! They're in the basket for decoration, not function!"

Which, honestly, seems to be a metaphor for my mother's life and my relationship with her.

We scratched our heads over these incidents, and Mom began to wonder if, maybe, she had a ghostly roommate in her new home. We both stopped wondering when one winter night in 2010, as we sat at her kitchen table working on a scrapbook, the dishwasher came on by itself. For a moment, we sat still and simply stared at one another.

"Does that thing have a timer?" I asked.

"Are you kidding?" she replied, "That thing has buttons for cleaning and drying. That's it. There's no timer anywhere. There aren't even any dishes inside it."

I got up, walked over, and opened the dishwasher, stopping the cycle. The wash button hadn't been activated, and we couldn't figure out how it had turned on by itself. Again, we opted for the breaker route and reset the kitchen switch, which quieted the dishwasher. We simply shook our heads and got back to work. I have to admit, though, that I was bit jealous of my mother in that moment. I wished that my dishwasher could turn on by itself… as well as load… and unload itself.

I have to give props to my mother. Through all of this activity, she dealt with it in stride. None of it seemed to bother her. Of course, we're talking about the same woman who stored her dead husband's and brother's-in-law ashes behind her bedroom door and dealt with my deceased father's footsteps every night for three months after his death.

But one month after the dishwasher incident, she was sitting on her red and gold couch, her back to the front door of her house. With a rerun of *Magnum, P.I.* playing on her television, she quietly worked on her latest craft project. It was late at night, and the neighborhood was quiet. Suddenly, she heard her locked front door open and footsteps move across the entrance floor. She understandably freaked out. When she got up to confront whoever had just walked into her house without knocking, only to find her front door closed and still locked and the entrance empty, she immediately called me and shouted, "Get your team over here, dammit!"

Our investigation at Mom's house was quiet until Clint broke her chair. It was an old wooden, straight-back chair that Mom inherited from Paw-Paw after his death. She had placed it in her upstairs hallway as decoration and used the seat to display an old black and white photo of me from the West Virginia State Fair. It was from a Wild West photo booth, and I was eight years old. The photographer swathed me in a too-big prairie dress, gave me an umbrella, and said, "Now, don't smile. They didn't smile in the olden days. Just look straight into my camera."

So, of course, when someone told eight-year-old me not to smile, what did I do? I tried really hard not to smile, which resulted in a "Who just farted?" face. I hated that picture. I felt bad that Clint sat on the spindly chair and broke it, but I was also thankful that there was no longer a display for the fart-face picture.

For the rest of the night, Clint sat gingerly on every other surface and stated that he felt a female spirit in the home, pacing back and forth, from the back window of the master bedroom to the front window in the master closet, watching everything going on in the neighborhood. He also sensed Civil War soldiers roaming on the property. While he felt that the woman was intelligent and able to interact with her surroundings, he said the Civil War soldiers were definitely residual.

As usual, we went through the house with our electromagnetic field detectors and found no out-of-the-ordinary EMF readings. The temperature in Mom's house was also normal, and as we set up our cameras and video recorder, we decided to split into two teams: one would go inside and investigate while the other stood in the driveway, munching on snacks and sipping coffee. Then, we would trade places.

I was on the first team with Jordan. Everything was quiet, and we didn't notice anything out of the ordinary until we sat in the living room and conducted an EVP session. Mom's living room is two-stories tall, and along the back wall is her open staircase to the second floor. The staircase landing on the second floor is open and looks down on the living room.

Jordan sat on the couch and I lounged in the loveseat across from him. As we quietly sat and asked our questions, a woman giggled from the second floor landing. We immediately jumped up and ran up the stairs to investigate. Even though we knew ourselves to be the only people in the house, we went through all five rooms just to be sure. They were, of course, devoid of life. Tammy, the only other woman on the investigation, was outside in the driveway, and the upstairs high-pitched giggle sounded nothing like her full-throated laughs.

Later, as we all piled back into the house and sat in the living room for a final EVP session, Steve pulled out his Ovilus, which we had used before, but which I was very skeptical about using. An Ovilus is an experimental device that combines an EMF meter with a word dictionary. The Ovilus will constantly read the surrounding electromagnetic field, take those readings and plug them into an algorithm—basically, a mathematical equation—and the number it generates is equated to a word in the device's dictionary. The idea is that the spirits talk to investigators by affecting the surrounding EM field. I am always skeptical of new equipment when the packaging says, "proprietary algorithm" meaning "We're not going to tell you how we put this together or what little bit of code we used to tell it which words to spit out." But, when the device in question was sitting on a shelf near five rabbit figurines and started spitting out the word "bunny" somewhat consistently, well then I may just agree that this Ovilus thing is pretty interesting. And that's just what it did that night

A week later, as I listened to my audio, I heard a strange sort of yodeling sound during our EVP session in Mom's sewing and craft room. We never whisper during our EVP sessions, and if we make any strange noises, such as a cough, burp, or sneeze, then we make note of it on the recorder—"Uh, yeah. Please note that Jordan just crop-dusted the room, and we'll be leaving for the next ten minutes." Never, have any of us ever yodeled during an investigation. Yet that's the sound I heard when put my headphones on, and it was the same sound my fellow investigators agreed they heard as well.

Is Mom's spirit a person who once lived in this house or on this property? Is she a long-dead member of our family or a friend who has already passed on? We have no clue. Unfortunately, she never gave us a message or said her name or gave us her story. This is by no means unusual, but it's certainly frustrating, especially when we, and our clients, want answers. The one thing I wanted my mother to understand was that she didn't need to get worked up about whatever, or whoever, was existing with her in her home. Even though Clint felt the presence of a woman looking out of the bedroom windows and Civil War soldiers marching across her yard, that didn't mean they were menacing or scary. After all, if the woman's spirit was intelligent, from her point-of-view Mom was moving into *her* house, reorganizing *her* rooms, and disrupting *her* afterlife. There had to be some sort of truce or understanding. So, Mom sat down, stated out loud that she understood she was the "new kid in town," but this was now JoAnne's home. The mystery lady was welcome to stay, but to please keep the heart-racing scares to a minimum. I was very proud of her, and she has, honestly, been a model client. Whenever other clients look at me, panicked, and beg, "What do I do? Do I have to move out of my house? I need you to get rid of this!" I tell them the story of my mother and her spirit roomie.

We haven't returned to Mom's house to investigate. Clint fixed her chair, the hated picture was returned to its surface, and Mom and her roomie have an armistice in place. A few items have been moved since then, but Mom just calmly acknowledges them, thanks her housemate, asks her to keep it down, and moves on with her life, just as her ghostly roommate moves on with her afterlife. And, somehow, they coexist just fine.

Except for the Georgia cockroaches. There's absolutely no peaceful coexistence there.

OUR HAUNTED HOME

I never wanted to live in a haunted house.

I know, right? Interestingly, it's never been one of my life's goals. I admit that I love investigating the paranormal, but I've never thought about what it would be like to actually live in a haunted house, to possibly deal with the day-to-day annoyance of items that have been moved or shadows flitting just outside my periphery. When I first started investigating, I would go to the client's home, commiserate with them over their activity, pat them on the shoulder, give them my best advice, and then return to my activity-free home where I would sleep without fear of a ghost waking me up in the middle of the night.

Well, I mean, I still had kids waking me up at all hours, moving things all over the house, leaving trails of socks and Cheerios down the hallways, and scaring the bejeezus out of me with random viral ailments. But that's parental, not paranormal.

After only a few months of investigating, my first at-home paranormal experience happened. It was the craziest thing, and I still, to this day, cannot adequately describe the whole-body chill I experienced. It was a typical day in the Dobson household: Tyler was at work, I was doing housework, the five-year-old twins were happily watching *Little*

Bear in the family room, and Jarrod was napping upstairs. I was in the kitchen, cleaning countertops and washing dishes. The phone would not stop ringing and the constant barrage of telemarketer phone calls was getting on my last nerve. Finally, the phone rang a fourth time, and when I answered the phone, I let out the rudest, nastiest "Hello!" I could muster.

The phone, pressed against my right ear, gave only silence, which was common for telemarketer phone calls. So, I shouted a second, even more frustrated "Hello!!" to receive a response. But, the response I received was wholly unexpected. In my left ear, as if someone was standing behind me and leaning forward, I heard a loud female voice, just like my own, practically shout, "Hello!?" Meanwhile, the phone line remained silent.

Of course, I immediately looked behind me to discover what I already knew: there was no one standing there. Jarrod was still upstairs, fast asleep. The twins were still on the couch, 15 feet away, watching their show, and *Little Bear*, a character voiced by a young girl, was doing all the talking from a TV screen in another room. I still, to this day, cannot explain what happened. I looked around, noted the bright spring sun streaming in from outside, took in the familiar surroundings of my beloved home and sanctuary, and felt, in that second, like a stranger.

I carefully hung up the phone, placed it back in its charging cradle, and continued with my housework, trying to focus on the TV show and not on what had just happened. Many times during our investigations we picked up voices that mimicked our own. It's not an uncommon occurrence, but for it to happen during midday, in my own home, in my own ear, was something for which I was unprepared.

The skeptic in me mulled over what had happened. *You're just tired. You have a lot on your plate. Three little kids! I'll bet you heard Mother Bear's voice on the show and she said "Hello!" and that's what it was. It's okay. It's nothing odd.*

But, when I went back later and watched that episode by myself, in my bedroom, Mother Bear didn't say "Hello!" nor did any other character on the show. And considering my daughter only stood waist-high, it couldn't have been her. I didn't have a ready answer.

Several months later, Stefanie came to my house to host a Mary Kay party. Everything was going swimmingly. There was lots of laughter and hijinks as we ladies made ourselves up and tried foundations, lipsticks, and eye shadows. Eventually, Stefanie moved her order forms and calculator to my living room, at the front of the house, and told everyone to come see her when they had decided what they wanted to order. She later told me that as she was sitting on the couch, looking down at her phone, she saw the shadow of someone walking through the foyer, on her right. She assumed it was one of us and, looked up, only to realize that no one was there. Being the calm paranormal investigator, she didn't make a big fuss of it. She just let me know when it was my turn to order. We both looked at each other, nodded our heads, looked into the foyer, and then continued the business transaction at hand. When she and the other guests left, I told Tyler what had happened. He promptly put his fingers in his ears and chanted, "Lalalalalalalalala!" as loudly as he could, and walked away.

My husband cracks me up.

For a long time after Stefanie's shadow, nothing happened, and I again brushed off what had occurred to her as nothing more than tricks of light and tired minds. That is until I held a gathering at my house. It was the premiere of a new season of *Ghost Hunters* and I invited the whole team over to hang out and watch what promised to be an engaging hour of television—edited down from a week's worth of footage, of course. As we piled into the living room, I noticed that Tammy kept looking over her right shoulder, through the foyer, toward the front door. I didn't think anything of it. I figured that headlights coming toward our house had her curiously checking out the window.

After everyone left and I began my post-party cleanup, the phone rang. It was Tammy, who promptly asked, "So, what's going on in your house?"

I replied, "Um, I'm cleaning?"

She plainly stated, "That's not what I'm talking about. What's with the old lady in your foyer?"

Tammy proceeded to tell me that she saw an older woman wandering in our foyer throughout the duration of our party. She wasn't a scary figure or a spirit out to harm us, she was just... there. I had no answer for her. I had no idea of who it could be, whether it was a long-dead relative, a friend, or someone connected to the house or property. Tammy chuckled and after I hung up the phone, I promptly ran upstairs to tell Tyler, who looked at me and said, "Nope! Don't want to hear it!"

But, here's the thing about my fellow team members who are sensitives: I tend to take what they say at face value and unless another sensitive corroborates what they say, it's not gospel. And that's how I treated Tammy's bit of information until the team Christmas party just a few months later. As my fellow team members wandered in and out of my dining room, filling up on food, drink, and cheer, Clint leaned over the table and whispered in my ear, "So, what's with the old lady in your foyer?"

I immediately shouted, "Is this some kind of joke you and Tammy have cooked up?!"

Clint was shocked. He had no idea what I was talking about, and I could tell by the look on his face that he was surprised by my outburst.

"No! What are you talking about? I never talked to Tammy about your house. What did she say?"

I told him about the *Ghost Hunters* premiere and Tammy's phone call shortly thereafter. He was stunned and so was I. Here it was, confirmation that someone was in my home and making herself known.

Later that night, I broke the news to Tyler.

"Clint confirmed it," I announced, mouth covered in toothpaste foam, leaning against the bathroom counter, "we've got a ghost."

Tyler, still actively brushing, looked at me with his eyes wide. "What?" he mouthed.

"Remember?" I gestured with my toothbrush, "The voice I heard and the shadow Stefanie saw? And that Tammy said she saw an old lady in our foyer? Well, Clint confirmed it today. He asked me about the old lady and who she was. He swore up and down he hadn't spoken to Tammy, and I believe him."

Now, Tyler isn't one who is prone to cussing. He's a good, genteel Southern man. But this time? I'm pretty sure I heard a muffled, "Sonuvabish!" as he spit out his toothpaste. He glanced at the shower and shouted, "She better not watch me getting naked every morning!"

I patted him on his shoulder and reassured him that even if she did watch him during his morning ablutions, that she probably enjoyed what she saw and wasn't at all put out.

Tyler was not amused.

For the longest time after all of this, the activity quieted. I wasn't worried about the spirit who had made herself at home here. After all, I only seemed to experience her presence intermittently, and none of it was threatening or scary. I even wondered if maybe something had followed me home after an investigation and made itself comfortable in my overly-purple house. This was entirely possible and has happened to other investigators. The activity never lasts more than a few days and quickly dissipates because the transient spirit has nothing to tie them here, and so they return to their point of origin. And possibly the woman Tammy and Clint experienced was the residual imprint of a relative. Because I was a busy mom and wife and without daily paranormal activity to remind me of her presence, I forgot about my resident ghost until another bright, spring day. It was two years after my first experience, and I was doing some housework.

As per usual I had my earbuds firmly in place and my new wave 80s music cranked. Yaz, New Order, Depeche Mode, and Erasure were the requirement of the day and the only thing getting me through daily housework. I had just finished vacuuming the foyer—dancing to "Blue Monday"—turned off the offending appliance, and removed my ear buds for a water break. Within seconds of the descent of blessed silence, I heard someone shout my name from upstairs. I was completely alone. The kids were in school, Tyler was at work, and it was just me, the cat, and the dog. And nowhere in the lyrics of New Order's "Blue Monday" is my name, or an approximation of my name—leather, feather, weather. "Heather" was shouted so clearly that before I could think about it, I responded with an exasperated, "What?!" When silence reasserted itself, I remembered that I was alone. I felt a little bad for replying so testily so I decided, for good measure, to walk around outside my house and make sure my neighbor wasn't calling my name. I found no one outside and no one was upstairs. I returned inside the house and shouted, "I'm sorry I responded that way! I hate housework!" I was worried my ghostly friend was a bit put out because of my terse response, and I wanted to make sure she didn't take it personally.

Again, many months passed with no paranormal happenings. With this kind of intermittent activity it was easy to forget about my freeloading houseguest. As a dutiful wife, though, I made sure to remind Tyler that she probably watched him take a shower every day. As per usual, he raised his eyebrows, looked at me with an exasperated expression, and replied, "You're not funny." Somehow, we're still married.

It was a cold, bleary November evening, when I was at my most relaxed, that she struck again. Tyler was out of town on a business trip, and I was eating dinner at the kitchen counter, the stairs leading up to the bedrooms off to my right. The kids had just finished eating and were on the kitchen floor behind me, playing with the dog, and that's when I heard it. A cough. Not some namby-pamby cough that the cat would make and can barely be heard over the HVAC, but a really loud, low, crackly cough. And it came from, you guessed it, upstairs. My fork was halfway to my mouth when it happened and, honestly, my fork stayed at that halfway point for a few minutes while I listened, carefully and hard, trying to hear anything from above. The kids were behind me, unaware of anything, rubbing the dog's belly and telling her what a good girl she was. I quietly excused myself with, "I need to go to the bathroom" and soundlessly climbed the stairs. I tiptoed into each room, making sure we were still the only four people in the house, and when I confirmed it, I sighed in relief. For me, a ghost is far better than a burglar. I whispered into the ether, "I heard you. I know you're here. Thanks for that. I need to finish my dinner, and put the kids to bed."

It's been three years since I've heard my old lady. Is she still here? I have no idea. She'll probably show back up at a moment when I least expect it and I'll, of course, let her know I heard her. We have a comfortable, quiet agreement—she doesn't touch my chocolate, and I don't kick her out—and I know that if she never makes another sound, I'll be simultaneously sad and relieved. Sad that my friend is gone, but relieved that she's finally moved on to her next adventure.

GHOSTLY VACATIONS

Tyler and I have been married for over twenty years, but we've
been a couple for over thirty. We have seen each other at our
best, worst, healthiest, sickest, happiest, and saddest. We've learned
the arts of compromise, tolerance, and patience. Our marriage works
and I foresee it lasting as long as we stick it out on this earthly plane.
Something I've discovered about Tyler is that it doesn't matter where
in the world we go, he will sniff out the nearest naval or aeronautical
museum for us to investigate old airplanes and battleships. He is happiest
when his six-foot, four-inch frame is bent over inside an old submarine
or crawling up into a derelict cargo plane, reading all the historical
placards informing the public how many battles the crew fought in.
Generally, old ships and planes aren't my cup of tea, but I gamely tag
along because I enjoy his enjoyment. And I also know that later, once
darkness falls, he will hesitantly go along on whatever ghost tour I've
booked for the two of us.

Many people decide to take a ghost tour because they expect to
see or experience something creepy. And that makes sense because the
ghost tours don't usually happen during the bright light of day. They
are scheduled after the sun goes down, and they make sure to take you

to the homes where murders occurred, to go past local cemeteries, and to show you the run-down buildings that look like set dressings for a horror movie. It's understandable why people expect to get scared on a ghost tour.

Actually, I've found that ghost tours are the gateway for a local history lesson. Interspersed between anecdotes of apparitions are stories of wars, love, people, and events both happy and sad. The tours are always entertaining, and because the history is presented as ghost stories, my interest is easily held and I learn more than I expected.

The first time I dragged Tyler along on a ghost tour, it was in New Orleans. It was 1997, our marriage was in its terrible twos, and our young 25-year-old brains had decided that Halloween in the Crescent City was an incredible idea. We were buzzed from the many drinks imbibed at Pat O'Brien's, and our tour guide looked more like a voo-doo priestess—and probably was—than a tour guide. We heard about murder, mayhem, love, and heartbreak in the Big Easy. I could imagine the streets filled with women wearing long dresses and men in top hats, the humidity slowing their steps, their words a mix of different languages and accents. The history of New Orleans came alive for us, and when we returned to its streets the next morning, chasing away our hangovers with café au lait and beignets, we had a greater respect for its past as well as its ghosts.

For our 20th anniversary, Tyler and I scrimped and saved for a dream trip to Hawai'i. Tyler, a long-time *Magnum, P.I.* fan, had fantasized driving the curvy, ocean roads of O'ahu since his childhood, and I had always wanted to explore the ocean waters around the islands. It was the perfect place for us to celebrate our special marriage milestone, and so we found ourselves, during the summer of 2015, soaking up the Pacific sun. Just two days after we landed, while our bodies were still adjusting to the six-hour time change, I reserved two spots on the "Orbs of O'ahu" tour with O'ahu Ghost Tours. Although our watches said 8 o'clock in the evening, our bodies insisted it was the wee morning hours of 2 a.m.

We stood on a side street on downtown Honolulu, waiting for a van to pick us up to take us on a driving tour of the island, showing us the most haunted spots. Tyler, yawning, shoved his hands in his pockets, and asked, "Why are we doing this again?"

"Because ghost reasons," I answered, mirroring his yawn. Just then, a van emblazoned with "O'ahu Ghost Tours" pulled to the curb in front of us, and our adventure began.

We first drove to the Nu'uanu Pali Lookout where we were buffeted by the strong winds whipping up the cliffs. As the wind howled, our tour guide loudly told us the story of King Kamehameha I and the battle of Nu'uanu, when his majesty united O'ahu under his leadership. The fighting was deadly, and many Hawai'ian solders lost their lives when they were forced off the cliffs. The guide told us the story of a female ghost that likes to lure men off the cliffs as well as the legend of the Mo'o, a lizard woman who protects the nearby waterfalls and will entice you off the cliffs to your death if you trespass near her waterfalls. I shivered from the cold wind, looking down on the lights of Kailua, my sleep-deprived brain sensing the spirit of Hawai'i.

Later, we stopped along the road and walked into the woods, hearing the story of a treacherous stretch of highway where many people lost their lives to the nearby hairpin turn and the ever-present wet pavement in this rainforest environment. As we listened to our guide, I could hear the cars passing behind us, imagining the many wrecks as they happened and hoping one wouldn't occur tonight. As we drove from location to location, Tyler and I would drift off, fitfully napping as the passenger van navigated the dark island roads. The other tour attendees quietly talked amongst themselves while we tried to catch up on needed sleep. We stopped at ancient burial sites, historic homes, and even a zoo, but then we ventured deep into the forest and heard the story of the nightmarchers.

The nightmarchers, or huaka'i pō, are the ghosts of ancient Hawai'ian warriors. These long-dead warriors march through the island, carrying torches, chanting or playing drums, their destination an ancient battleground. Those who happen upon the nightmarchers and don't pay the proper respect by lying prone on the ground and keeping their eyes down may lose their lives. As I stood behind Tyler, the trees swaying behind me and raindrops hitting the arboreal canopy above me, I scanned our surroundings, listening for the far-off sounds of drums and looking for torchlight between the branches.

Thankfully, the nightmarchers didn't make an appearance, but as I stood at the back of the group, I heard my name whispered in my left ear... except there was no one there. No one stood behind or beside me. As the chills raced up my spine, Tyler turned, sensing the change in my posture which had gone from relaxed to tense. He looked at me, questioningly, and I simply smiled and silently thanked the Hawai'ian spirits for welcoming me to their beautiful island.

Two years after our Hawai'ian adventure, Tyler and I planned a long weekend getaway for just the two of us. His parents graciously took the kids for several days, and we decided on Savannah as our destination of choice. We couldn't wait to go. And then Tyler asked me a loaded question.

"Where should we stay?"

Having been married to a paranormal investigator for 22 years, he should have known the answer that would fly from my mouth.

"Let's stay in a haunted hotel!"

When Tyler and I first got married, we spent our honeymoon in Seattle, Washington. Rather than spending our first week in wedded bliss at a Hilton or a Hyatt, we stayed at two different bed and breakfasts. The first was a mid-century modern home in the hills above Seattle. The kitschy furnishings made us feel like we had stepped backward into the Brady Bunch house, and the couple who owned the home ate breakfast with us each morning and pointed out the sights we should see. It was such a personal touch that most hotels seem to be missing. From that point on, Tyler and I felt that staying small was the way to go. Once

I started investigating the paranormal, I knew that *haunted* bed and breakfasts were the way to go. Having the opportunity to be awakened in the middle of the night by a ghost became a bonus I couldn't deny myself. Tyler, though, was happy to pass up that singular experience.

The place we chose was the Marshall House on Broughton Street. Mary Marshall, a Savannah businesswoman of the 19th century, realized that with the fast growth of the town in the 1840s and 1850s due to the railroad boom, the town was in need of hotels and boarding houses. The Marshall House was built in 1851 and housed wounded Union soldiers at the end of the Civil War and was also used as a hospital during the Yellow Fever Epidemics of 1854 and 1876. It operated for over 100 years until it was closed in 1957 due to structural problems on the second, third, and fourth floors. Even though it no longer operated as a hotel, shopkeepers still rented the first floor up until 1998, when the entire building was closed for extensive renovations and reopened a year later, again becoming a grand hotel. Throughout its history, residents, guests, and patients have experienced ghostly encounters that include the sounds of children running up and down the hallways at night, faucets turning on by themselves, and shadows in the foyers. I don't know what I was hoping to encounter, but in Savannah, Georgia, a town full of rich history and ghosts, I was hoping for something to at least pat me on the shoulder. Poor Tyler, on the other hand, located a nearby Holiday Inn Express and announced that if he saw or heard anything, he would be spending the rest of our vacation ensconced there. I scoffed.

When we arrived at the Marshall House, I fell in love with the period furnishings and the 160-year-old bannister and stairwell. Walking up the stairs to our second-floor room, the steps creaked at all the right moments, the wood under my hands was velvet-smooth from thousands of other hands running along the surface for over a century. Tyler returned downstairs to take care of the luggage while I took in our beautiful room with its long, floral drapes and century-old wooden floor. I spoke out loud to the room and said, "I don't know if you're here or if you're listening, but I want you to know my name is Heather. I'm a friend, and if you want to visit me while I'm here, that will be just fine."

Nothing obliged me. No objects were moved, no shadows were seen, and no disembodied voices were heard. All in all, it was a quiet four nights. Broughton Street, it turns out, is a very busy place during a warm spell just before Thanksgiving. Outside our window, we could hear students from the Savannah College of Art and Design enjoying ice cream from the parlor across the street while residents and out-of-town guests strolled through the shops, stocking up on Christmas gifts. Each day when dawn broke, I wondered if any other guests in the hotel had experienced late-night visitors from the Marshall's history.

But, our attempts at ghostly contact didn't just end with our hotel room. On a bright afternoon, we stopped by the Moon River Brewery, a local watering hole famous for not only its beer but also its ghost stories. At the crowded bar, we tried to make sense of the soccer game playing on the TV above us while we sampled their brews, downed burgers, and gamely waited for a voice in our ears or a flitting shadow in the corner. The spirits were delicious, but the ghosts were uncooperative.

And, of course, we took a local ghost tour. At sundown on our last night, we waited on a dark street corner for our tour guide to arrive. Tyler was convinced that the next two hours were a huge mistake. I, of course, told him to shush and triple-checked the location of the tour's starting point. Eventually, other tour goers and our guide arrived, walking out of the darkness and joining us under the lone street lamp. For the next two hours, we walked through historic neighborhoods beneath stately oak trees dripping with Spanish moss. We quietly padded through a local cemetery, full of people who helped make Savannah the town it is today, and heard about modern-day ghosts as well as those who have been around since the founding of the city in 1733. At the end of the tour, we stood in front of a beautiful, yet abandoned, home. According to the tour guide, its story was a tragic one, full of murder, heartbreak, and many ghostly happenings. All I know is that house spoke to me and if I had had the money, I would have immediately written out a check for its purchase.

When we eventually packed our bags and returned home, Tyler was relieved that our stay had been ghost-free. I, on the other hand, though rested and now in love with this gorgeous city, was saddened that we hadn't been graced with the presence of even one ghost. Though we couldn't say that the spirits of Savannah graced us, we can definitely say that the spirit of Savannah herself was with us every moment of our visit there.

I love taking ghost tours, visiting haunted locations, and walking amongst a city's history. No matter where we go, humanity has lived, loved, toiled, and died before our visit there. There are so many stories to hear, and I know that as our lives move forward, Tyler and I will continue to explore old ships, broken-down airplanes, and haunted places.

TRIGGERED

I'd rather be the devil, to be that woman man
I'd rather be the devil, to be that woman man

As the falsetto voice and twangy guitar of bluesman Skip James echoed throughout the second floor of Waverly Hills Sanatorium, the scratching of the needle across Jordan's record added to the ethereal mood of the evening. The sun had set over the horizon, creating a stunning light show of oranges and dark blues across the sky. Steve and I set out down the long hallway, past broken doors, and peeling paint, Skip's voice following us into the dark recesses of the once-grand, now decaying, hospital.

Two hours before, we had driven up an isolated driveway, the trees creating a canopy on either side of our cars. As our vehicles navigated the gravel and potholes, we craned our necks, trying to see the building through the vegetation. At last, we reached a metal gate and called the caretaker's number, letting her know we had arrived. As we waited to gain entry to the Waverly Hills property, we all stood at the entrance, mouths parted in awe, our voices silent. Before us stood a monstrous building, shaped like the letter "V," the angle more obtuse than acute.

Four stories with huge, gaping windows stared back at us, seeming to dare us to enter. A large, life-sized concrete gargoyle stood guard near the building, a testament to the building's colorful recent past when it served as a haunted house venue. The once-expansive driveway was covered in weeds as tall as my waist, and the facade was in need of a deep pressure wash. Rotting windows shared space with new, clean windows, the long-promised renovations slowly taking over the structure. As we took it all in, Tina Mattingly, the building's new owner, greeted us with a set of keys.

"Hey there!" she brightly exclaimed. "You must be Heather!"

"You are right!" I extended my hand. "We are all so thrilled to be here!"

"Well, come on in and let's get this party started with a quick tour and then you can start investigating!"

Tina made sure to show us everything on the property. She pointed out the operating rooms on the second, third, and fourth floors at the end of each long hallway. She showed us the patient rooms and the long, wide solarium hallways that were open to the fresh air and sunshine with only copper screens in place to keep the insects outside. We looked in on the morgue, the electroshock therapy room, the cafeteria, and the body chute, taking in everything with wide eyes and a multitude of questions. We couldn't wait for the night to begin.

Now, two hours later, our flashlights sliced through the still, dusty air, illuminating the decay all around us. We could hear the far-off footsteps of our other team members, also roaming the halls. As we walked, quietly listening, Jordan sat guard next to his record player. He wasn't playing Skip James for his own edification. He was playing it for the spirits of Waverly Hills.

Aw, nothin' but the devil, changed my baby's mind
Was nothin' but the devil, changed my baby's mind

Majestic on its hilltop, the city of Louisville just a stone's throw away, Waverly Hills stood isolated from everyone and everything. The beautiful building has not only stood the test of time but also the high emotion of sickness and death. It is a place revered by paranormal investigators and feared by the general public because of the reputation many in the field have given it. Turn on any paranormal reality TV show, and the stars will speak of the infamous body chute, the scary-sounding electroshock therapy room, and the morgue with hushed, terrified tones. But, despite the spurious stories and the sadness of disease, Waverly Hills Sanatorium isn't what it seems. It's not a structure full of evil and bad intentions. Instead, it was a witness to medical miracles and now is gaining a new lease on life thanks to the paying public and her caretakers.

I laid down last night, laid down last night
I laid down last night, tried to take my rest

Skip's voice sang on, his guitar adding to the loneliness of the place, the scratching of the needle against the record making me feel like I was walking the halls of Waverly Hills in the 1920s, not 2011. Many paranormal investigators hypothesize that mimicking the conditions the dead experienced when they were living can sometimes entice them to interact with us. We knew that before the advent of streptomycin in 1946, the modern-world antibiotic which nearly cured tuberculosis, also known as "consumption," TB was a wasting disease that reached its peak of infection in the 19th and early 20th centuries. By the 1800s, 40% of all working-class deaths were due to tuberculosis. Those ill with the disease were placed in sanatoria like Waverly Hills where, it was hoped, the disease would be contained. Because the cure at the time was fresh air and sunshine, many of these facilities, like Waverly Hills, were built with the aforementioned copper screens along the front of the structure. Patients were wheeled out in their beds or wheelchairs to take in the sunlight and breeze in these open-air solariums in the hopes that would cure them. As they sat out in the elements, they would talk, but only if permitted by the staff since it was believed that talking could exacerbate their illness. Otherwise, they could work on crafts, read, and listen to music on record players. Jordan, our resident historian and music expert, was playing his old blues records on a 21st century portable record player to create a familiar atmosphere in which the Waverly Hills spirits may want to communicate with us. Jordan's degree in history and his experience playing in various bands throughout his younger years placed him in a unique position to dig deeper into the historical stories of the sites we investigated. And he was excited to use music on this investigation to entice whatever spirits may be at Waverly Hills to come out and interact with us.

> *My mind got to ramblin', like a wild geese*
> *From the west, from the west*

Steve and I slowly made our way back to the center of the floor where Jordan and his record player were located. By now, the remaining light from the sun had completely disappeared over the horizon, and we were plunged into darkness save for the light from our flashlights. I shivered in my coat, wishing it wasn't an unseasonably cold April night. Suddenly, Steve's head whipped left, and his flashlight zeroed in on a doorway.

"Did you see that?" he harshly whispered.

"No!" I replied. "What did you see?"

"A shadow, peeking out at us from that door," he motioned with his chin.

We quickly walked to the doorway in question, sweeping our flashlights over the walls and into the corners. Even though our flashlights killed any shadow that may have been lurking there, we wanted to make sure no one was trying to play a trick on us. As we scanned the room, we realized there was no exit other than the door we walked through. That meant the shadow Steve had seen wasn't created by a living being.

"I think," I whispered, "the music is working."

Steve nodded his head in agreement.

The woman I love, woman that I loved
Woman I loved, took her from my best friend

Trigger objects can be useful things. Like the music Jordan was playing on the second floor solarium of Waverly Hills, a trigger object can be anything. It can be a doll that was well loved by the deceased, a letter from a loved one read out loud, a person walking through the halls of a hospital wearing a doctor's coat and stethoscope. If an investigator knows what type of haunting they're dealing with and who may be doing the haunting, then it's entirely possible to draw out the spirit with something they may have enjoyed while they lived. Though Skip James's song wasn't recorded until 1967, "Devil Got My Woman" and many other blues songs like it were traditional songs sung by any and all blues musicians. Originating with African-American musicians in the 19th century, the blues became a staple of 1920s music for both African- and white-Americans. It was our hope that Jordan's blues record would remind the since-passed patients of Waverly Hills of happier times.

But he got lucky, stoled her back again
And he got lucky, stoled her back again

Slowly, Steve and I drew closer to the solarium where Jordan was stationed. We could hear the shuffling of the other members of our team ahead of us and to our right. Suddenly, I heard an extra set of footsteps, but behind us. I stopped and signaled for Steve to do the same. Even though we were still, the footsteps behind us continued for a few steps more, and then halted. We looked at one another, turned around, and shined our flashlights down the long hall from whence we just came.

As expected, no one was there.

We glanced at one another, smiled, and continued on toward Jordan. The music was *definitely* working.

For me, Waverly Hills isn't an evil place or a building full of negativity as the paranormal reality shows would have us believe. It's actually a place of sadness. It's the knowledge that entire families were once infected by this horrible disease. Many families—mothers, fathers, and children—were all sent to sanatoriums in the hopes of being cured. Some did, with half of active tuberculosis patients surviving the disease. The other half could die within five years or less, depending on their age and the health of their immune systems. Once active in the body, tuberculosis is a horrible wasting illness. As Steve and I rounded the corner and saw Jordan, we quietly signaled our presence and waited for the other members of the team to join us.

As I stood there, waiting for Jordan's record to finish, I couldn't help but wonder how it would feel to bring my children here, for their lives to be contained to a playground on the roof of a gigantic building full of seriously ill people, many of them dying each day. I thought back to the one spring when Heath had been hit by a mystery illness. As his fever kept spiking and the doctors kept throwing antibiotics at him while shrugging their shoulders, I was finally at my wit's end after two weeks. I ultimately confronted the doctor and said, "That's it. He's missed nine days of school, and he's miserable. I don't care what it takes! Blood work! X-Rays! Whatever! Let's do it to figure out what he's got!" Several hours, one needle stick and two X-Rays later, we had our diagnosis: walking pneumonia. I was so very relieved to have an answer and to know he was sick with something that was fixable with modern-day medicines. Here we were, in the 21st century, taking home a bottle of pills and a carton of rainbow sherbet where Heath would recover with his favorite TV shows and stuffed animals. The children of Waverly Hills, sickened with tuberculosis, weren't so lucky. Knowing that humbled me to my core.

Just as Skip's voice gave way to the scratching of the needle against the center of the record, the rest of our team wandered back into the second floor solarium. Jordan carefully put his record away, unplugged the record player, and stood up.

"Well?" he asked, "What do you guys think?"

Steve smiled, "Brilliant."

We carried Jordan's record player back down to the visitor's center, located in a separate building, where we could eat, store our valuables, and warm up. Once gathered, we broke up into multiple teams and decided who would investigate where for the night. And what a night it was. For eight solid hours, each team made their way through the entire building, investigating the morgue, the fourth floor operating room, patient rooms, darkened hallways, and the notorious, spider web-filled body chute. Every two hours, we met back in the main office, broke into our snacks, filled each other in on what had happened, and decided where each team would go next. Nancy had spread herself out on a morgue table while Jordan tried to coax a doctor into responding to him in an operating room. Stefanie communed with any spirits that may have been in the body chute while I sat in the solarium, listening for any sound that shouldn't be there. Shadows flitted in and out of our peripheral visions and unexplained noises plagued our ears. At no time did I feel like we were the only ten people in that massive structure. In fact, it felt like crowds of people constantly surrounded us, watching, waiting for the right opportunity to speak.

Eventually, my team made it to the fifth floor. Essentially, the fifth floor was much smaller than the rest of the sanatorium. It was the roof of the main building with two patient rooms, able to house around 20 patients total, as well as a nurse's office and a playground set. Taking up the center of the roof, the fifth floor was where the children and the most serious adult cases were housed. The medical community of the time felt that those people most needed access to the fresh air and sunlight, and where better to receive both of those things than to be wheeled out onto the roof of the building. The children were provided with a swing set, and we knew this because pictures on display in the office show afflicted children playing on the roof, swinging in the sunshine, while nurses watched over them. It was in the children's room—now a large, empty room with paint peeling from the walls and water stains dotting the ceiling—that we set up our K2 meter, hoping for communication with whatever was there. I wanted whoever was there to feel at ease, so I made myself small, like a child, and spoke softly. I crouched down close to the meter and began talking.

"Hi there!" I said brightly, wanting any children that may be there to feel comfortable with my presence. "My name is Heather! Will you tell me your name? I have a recorder here with a bright red light. If you get close to it and say your name, I'll be able to hear you when I listen to it later!"

I then pointed to the K2 meter. "Do you see this little thing? With the pretty green light? Did you know that if you pass your hand through it, you can make the lights change from green to orange to red? Isn't that neat?" I turned the meter off and then back on, making the lights flash as the device reset, showing whoever was there how the lights could change. I continued in my best mom-of-preschoolers-voice, "If you do that, then I can ask you some questions. If the answer is 'Yes' then you can wave your hand through the lights, and I'll see them change! If the answer is 'No' then don't do anything at all. Let's play, okay?"

The K2 meter light immediately changed from green to red, and I knew that whoever was there wanted to communicate. And so, I began asking questions.

"Were you sick?"

The K2 meter lit up to orange and then changed back to green.

"Were you a child?"

Again, the lights changed to orange.

"I have some toys downstairs. Would you like me to bring them upstairs for you to play with?"

The K2 lights flashed to red in quick succession as if something was trying to communicate in Morse code.

"Okay, okay! I have some toy cars. Would you like those to play with?"

The K2 lights remained stubbornly on green.

"Are you sure?" I reiterated. "They're really nice metal cars. My son loves playing with them."

Again, the K2 light remained steady on green and unresponsive. Clearly, whoever was there wasn't interested in Hot Wheels.

"Or, maybe you would like to play with a tea set?"

The K2 emphatically blinked to red.

"Excellent! I'm going to go downstairs now and bring the tea set back upstairs. Okay?"

I turned off the meter, set off on the long trek back to the visitors area, and retrieved the bag with Amelia's small tea set. I added a Sharpie marker and a large piece of butcher paper. When I returned to the fifth floor, I set the paper on the bare concrete floor and arranged the miniature ceramic tea set on the paper. With the large teapot in the center and two teacups and saucers on either side, I made sure to place the sugar and creamer bowls nearby. I fished the teapot's lid out of the bag and placed it on the teapot's opening. After getting everything arranged just so, I used the Sharpie marker to trace around the bottom of each item, marking where I had placed them.

"Okay," I announced, "if you're still here, I'm going to leave this until morning. You're free to play with it as much as you like, but please be careful because it's my daughter's and I don't want it to break. See you later, and have fun!"

And I left my trigger objects, hoping the little girl spirit I felt was still on the fifth floor would enjoy playing without interruption. I returned to my team and asked them to leave the fifth floor alone, to not go up for several hours, so that no human movement or contamination would interfere with whatever was there.

As we continued our investigation at Waverly Hills, I walked through it with the mind of a parent, wondering how I would feel if my children were patients here, and I visited the three of them on the fifth floor. Then I wondered how I would feel if I had to stay here myself after leaving my children behind in the care of relatives or friends. Would I be optimistic and happy during my time here, or would I lie in my bed, having already given up? I recalled the month I spent on bed rest while pregnant with Amelia and Heath. During the early days of that month, I was actually rather excited. Tyler would have to wait on me hand and foot, and I wouldn't have to cook or do laundry or any other mundane housework. I could surf the Internet, cross-stitch the many baby projects I had stacked up, and watch all the TV my eyes could handle. After just a few days, though, lying in bed wore on me. It was monotonous, boring, and seemingly never-ending. Friends would come visit and tell me about the craft shows they attended, the latest movies they saw, and the weather. And all I could think about was how much I wanted to be out there with them. Being that way for a month was pretty awful. I couldn't imagine being that way for years. My mother would tell the story of how she contracted Asian flu while in high school and fell so ill with such severe respiratory problems that she was nearly sent to a sanatorium in Virginia. I'm sure that prospect put fear in the hearts of my grandparents.

Our EVP sessions that night ran the gamut of topics. We tried reaching out to the tuberculosis patients, doctors, and nurses of the early 20th century, asking questions like:

"Were your children ill, and did they stay here alongside you?"

"When you performed a thoracoplasty, did you prefer removing two or three ribs in order to collapse the lung, or did it depend on the patient and the severity of their condition?"

"How many geriatric patients were in minimally conscious states versus alert and aware of their surroundings?

"Did the color of the sputum reflect the severity of the patient's tuberculosis case?"

"Were any procedures in place to minimize sarcopenia in the geriatric patients?"

"What was the success rate of lobectomies versus a thoracoplasties? Did you find that removing lung tissue was more or less successful than collapsing the lung?"

And to the geriatric patients and their caregivers of the latter part of the century, we asked: "Were you abused by the doctors and nurses here at Woodhaven Geriatric Center?"

Several times, we heard doors creak open and saw movement where there shouldn't have been. Once, on the fourth floor, our K2 meter signaled an intelligent presence that directly answered our questions about abuses when Waverly Hills operated as the Wood Haven Geriatric Hospital and housed elderly residents in the 1980s. The "Yes" answers it gave to our pointed questions regarding neglect, beatings, and psychological abuse were incredibly heartbreaking. In other areas, like the morgue, cafeteria, and the body chute—where supplies from trains at the bottom of the hill were brought into the hospital and bodies of those patients who had passed were taken out—the K2 meter stayed silent, not budging from the green light it faithfully displayed when turned on.

As morning dawned, Steve and I returned to the fifth floor to retrieve Amelia's tea set. There, still on the floor, on top of the paper, sat every piece I had laid down. Except now, I noticed that the teapot and creamer bowl had been moved because they no longer lined up with the tracings I had made on the paper. Steve and I looked at each other, eyebrows raised. Clearly, someone had poured themselves some pretend tea and milk from the ceramic tea set. We carefully gathered up the items, wrapped them in the towel I had brought them in, and placed them in my bag, the clinking of the ceramic the only noise on the 5th floor. This tea set had, in one night, become very special and I knew, right then, that I would never be able to tell Amelia what had happened because she would never play with it again. I looked around the room and announced to whomever was there, "We hope you enjoyed playing tea time! We'll bring it back the next time we come."

Waverly Hills wasn't this death trap on a hill that so many paranormal reality stars want us to think it was. It's an incredibly stately building that is slowly, but surely, being transformed from the rotting, crumbling hulk it has become back into the gorgeous structure it once was. The owners hope to one day turn Waverly Hills into a beautiful hotel. The money we spent—$100 per person—touring and investigating Waverly Hills went back into restoring the building to its former glory so that it may one day house guests in comfort and luxury.

Waverly Hills is a strange mix of the sadness of death and the joy of a cure that eradicated an ancient disease. It has embraced the living and the dead, all while standing silently atop a hill overlooking Louisville and the Ohio River. So many people have called for Waverly Hills's destruction, citing that it is a building that has outlived its usefulness. But, I think that Waverly Hills is a memory that needs to stay within sight of our collective consciousness. We need to remember the days of disease and hope, of pre-antibiotics and experimental medicine. We need to walk those silent halls that no longer ring with the cacophony of rattling coughs and to sit in those quiet rooms that hold the secrets of those once housed there. We need to stand at the wide windows and breathe in the fresh, Kentucky air and soak in the southern sun, just as those patients did so long ago. And as we do, we need to think of those people who stayed there, and wonder if he or she made it home to their family or if they passed beyond the veil and watch us still. We need to understand that not all is as it seems.

ALL GOOD THINGS

J ust like life, the sun, and the universe, everything has an end. Sometimes, the endings are sad, unexpected, and unwelcome. Other times, the endings are exciting and desirable, giving us an opportunity to change our static lives into something more dynamic. Atlanta Paranormal Investigations was something I never wanted to end, but when it did, I helped close the door myself, and I was happy to do it.

From the moment I joined, I felt that I was never quite good enough for Atlanta Paranormal, that I was a placeholder until the founders could find someone better. Darlene made sure to remind us, many times, that there were hundreds of people lined up to join our group and that we were lucky to be there, that we could be replaced at any time. That statement, very casually thrown around, made me feel that I was expendable. Our small group of newly-minted investigators—Clint, Jordan, Stefanie, Tammy, and I—all felt irritated that we did the work of interviewing clients, setting up appointments, conducting investigations, combing through hundreds of hours of audio and video footage for evidence, doing all the paperwork, and writing final reports, even visiting courthouses to do property research, yet received little to no thanks from our founders who made sure to always mention themselves in newspaper articles and news interviews.

The straw that broke the camel's back was when the cast of *Ghost Hunters* decided to focus an episode of their show on two sites in the Atlanta area. Darlene and her husband, of course, took part in the show and were on camera for the full hour-long episode. None of us were even allowed to show up, meet the very people who had inspired us to become paranormal investigators—Jason Hawes and Grant Wilson, the founders of The Atlantic Paranormal Society and stars of *Ghost Hunters*—or simply thank them. We were summarily dismissed by Darlene and told to stay away and not bother them. It was a kick in the head. After all our work at making Atlanta Paranormal a success, this was how we were rewarded. Our behind-the-scenes grumbling turned to full-blown complaints 18 months after beginning our involvement with Atlanta Paranormal, and we finally realized it was time to strike out on our own.

We met at a local Mexican restaurant to make sure we were on the same page, that we truly wanted to take on the monster task of starting our own group. The biggest obstacle, of course, was getting our name out there with absolutely no advertising budget and no experience in sales. It's hard to persuade people to allow you to investigate their claims of paranormal activity when they've never heard of you, and you have no one to recommend you. Luckily, I had been a blogger for two years and knew a bit about social media and how to rig a website to place our name in the top of search engine lists. But, it wouldn't happen overnight and would be a months-long, possibly years-long, process.

First, though, we needed a name. Jordan immediately spoke up.

"No way are we doing some stupid name with an acronym! Like G.H.O.S.T. or S.P.I.R.I.T!"

"Aw, come on, J-Walk," I cajoled. "You don't want us to be known as the Georgia Haunted Otherworld Spirit Team? Or how about the Southern Paranormal Investigative Research Inquiry Team?"

"I swear, H-Bomb," Jordan replied, "if y'all pick some stupid name like that, I'm walking. I'm out of here. The only team that is *ever* allowed to have an acronym as their name is Rhode Island Paranormal. R.I.P. is okay. But that's it."

"Well," Clint said, "since we're a long way from Rhode Island, I guess that name is completely out of the question."

"I don't know," Tammy said, "I think we should go for it. We'd certainly stand out from all the Georgia, Southeastern, and Southern teams."

I laughed so hard that I snorted, and Jordan just looked at all of us with veiled contempt on his face.

After lots of talking, arguing, and numerous bowls of chips and salsa, we all finally agreed on Paranormal Georgia Investigations. It was short, sweet, to the point, and demonstrated that we were willing to travel statewide to investigate. Plus? No one else was using that name, which was a huge bonus. Immediately, we all whipped out our phones, connected to the Internet, and began reserving the necessary website domain names, Facebook accounts, and Twitter handles. This was going to be a huge undertaking and before we even formally left our old group, we had to get the new one off the ground. As we parted from the restaurant, we agreed on a date and time to meet with Darlene and her husband, and we knew that the end was nigh.

Of course, I was going through my own drama at the time. My next-door neighbor had roped me into serving on my neighborhood's homeowners' association.

"Aw, come on, Heather!" she begged. "It will only be for a year! Michael resigned, and we need a Secretary to fill in until elections in January!"

After a week of her sad puppy-dog eyes and pouty lips, I agreed, not because I had a sense of duty, but because I'm very susceptible to guilt. Eventually, my year-long stint at taking notes became a full-blown battle against the HOA vice-president who was a complete bully, prone to violent outbursts and threats. My neighbor—the HOA president—and

I could do nothing but hold on with our fingernails and try to make it to January without responding to his intimidation tactics. Combine this with being a full-time mom to three children under the age of four, not a lot of sleep, and the impending confrontation with Darlene, and I was a complete basket case.

When the day dawned to meet with our Atlanta Paranormal founders, I was fielding phone calls from the HOA president.

"Heather, we need to stop going to meetings," she said. "If Paul doesn't have quorum, then he can't pass any business and can no longer bully us."

"True, Jodi," I replied, "but can we talk when I get home? I've got something going on right now."

"Oh, sure!" she said, "No problem! We're totally going to nail his ass!"

As we walked up to Darlene's door, my phone rang again. This time, it was Sarah, another member of the HOA board.

"Heather! You and Jodi absolutely cannot antagonize Paul any further!" she practically shouted.

"I'm not antagonizing anyone, Sarah!" I forcefully replied. "I'm just trying to let a bully know that he can no longer intimidate and threaten me or my friend! What he's doing is wrong and I won't allow him to do it any further! You go ahead and roll over if you like, but I won't! And I'm going into an important meeting right now! Please don't call again!"

By the time we stepped into Darlene's house, I was shaking. My nerves were shot, and all I wanted at that very moment was a corner where I could cry and release every pent-up emotion I was feeling. And then eat chocolate. In the end, our meeting with Darlene and her husband went as well as we could have hoped. We tried to make our grievances known, that we would love to stay with Atlanta Paranormal if we could run it and be the faces of the group, with them stepping back in supportive rolls, but they refused. This was their organization, and she demanded to be the face, name, and voice of it, regardless of whether she did the work or not. And so we resigned.

As we walked out of their house, Clint asked Darlene's husband, "Hey, can we grab the cameras we paid for?" and for some reason, that upset me. I began to cry. The emotions of the day had become too much for me, and all the anger and sadness and fatigue I had held in check came bubbling up.

Jordan hugged me, a confused look on his face, and patted my back. "It'll be okay, H-Bomb." The rest of the group gathered around me, offering words of comfort and hugs. Even Darlene's husband gave me a hug, and that just made me cry even harder. These people were my family. In 18 short months they had become an important part of my life, and I absolutely loved them for it. Even though we would still be investigating together, saying goodbye to the people who gave me a chance to investigate was hard.

Slowly, but surely, we constructed our website, ordered business cards, and cranked up our social media presence. "Search engine optimization" became words I would repeat ad nauseam at our monthly meetings. In the midst of begging friends and family for investigation opportunities, I was gradually moving our name up in the Google search statistics.

Our proudest moment, though, was the day our shirts came in. Part of becoming a full-fledged investigator with Atlanta Paranormal Investigations was getting to wear the team shirt with the group logo on the front and the website listed on the back. I wore that shirt at every investigation, every event, and every meeting. I was so very proud to be a paranormal investigator with Atlanta Paranormal that I even wore it on Halloween. I was proud of it until I realized that same pride didn't extend to the founders. When our Paranormal Georgia Investigations shirts were delivered, it was a different kind of pride. This was a group I helped found, a group I took so much joy in. I had given input on the logo, I had built the website, and I was part owner, essentially, of this organization. I wore that shirt not just to investigations and meetings, but also to the grocery store, the PTA, and date nights with Tyler. With

"PARANORMALGEORGIA.COM" emblazoned across the back, it was free advertising, and I wore it until the black faded to a charcoal gray and the embroidered moon on the front became frayed. I was more proud of that shirt than any designer blouse in my closet.

What I first thought was a tragic ending was actually an exciting beginning. And isn't that what life is all about? One moment we're all riding a high wave of joyous accomplishment, and the next minute our lives are unexpectedly turned upside down. The sky is the limit, and then you're in the crapper. That's what I felt like when we left API. But then, along came our little group PGI. And I haven't come down from out of the clouds yet.

Of course, poor Jordan and his hate for acronym names came back to haunt him when seven years later I investigated an abandoned hospital with three fellow female investigator friends. We signed up for the night's activities under the pseudonym "T.W.A.T.S."—The Women's All-night Terror Squad. We giggled, snorted, and took a picture of the sign we made, sent it to Jordan, and eagerly awaited his reply. He was not amused but did inquire as to when we were having our team shirts made. It's become a running joke ever since, but I have yet to build up the chutzpah to have such a shirt made. The Bible Belt tends to frown on such things.

THE BEGINNING

I remember taking my mother to see *The Fellowship of the Ring* in the movie theater. Like many people the world over, I had read the books and was aware of the magnitude of this moment. J.R.R. Tolkien's work was finally being given the theatrical treatment it deserved. It was going to be agony waiting for the releases of the other two movies, but it was going to be worth it. As the final scene of the movie faded to black and credits started rolling, my mother just stared at the screen.

"Right?!" I exclaimed. "Wasn't that amazing?"

"It was... good." She replied. "But, it ended kind of funny."

"What do you mean?"

"Well, we have no idea if they returned the ring! I mean, it just... ended right in the middle of the story!"

Realization dawned. Apparently, my mother had been living in a literature black hole and had never read *The Lord of the Rings* trilogy or even heard of J.R.R. Tolkien.

"Mom!" I exclaimed, "It's the first of a trilogy! There's two more books, and there will be two more movies! We still have *The Two Towers* and *The Return of the King* to go!"

"OH! Okay. That makes more sense."

I bring this up because you're probably making the same face my mom made in that movie theater. You're flipping further along, trying to find another chapter, and wondering if the publisher stiffed you.

I assure you, neither the publisher nor myself cheated you out of part of this book. When I started writing *Memoirs of a Future Ghost* in November, 2016, it began as a collection of short essays, then—thanks to the guidance of my editor Wayne—morphed into more of a cohesive story which itself evolved as he edited and I re-wrote. One morning, I looked down at the word count, saw a number very close to 110,000 words, channeled Keanu Reeves, and thought, "Whoa."

Tyler, my ever-patient husband and lover of all things that come in threes—*Star Wars*, the aforementioned *Lord of the Rings*, *Indiana Jones*, and our three kids—suggested, "Why don't you break your book up into two books? Then, you'll have time to write a third book and have a trilogy."

I fully admit that I gave him the ol' stink-eye and sarcastically replied, "Oh, yeah, sure, great idea, George Lucas!" And then I stewed on it and realized he was correct. Even though we have three children, two of them are twins and one is a singleton. Why not do the same with my books? Make this first book a set of two and then write a third?

What I'm trying to tell you is that "All Good Things" isn't the end of this journey. There is a second book that picks up where this one leaves off. It continues my adventures along with those of Clint, Stefanie, Jordan, Tammy, Steve, and a few new people. And after that second book, there will be a third. Just because I've finished writing doesn't mean I'm done investigating. There are so many more stories to be told, so many more paranormal occurrences to investigate. And I won't leave you hanging. So, like any good film production company, I leave you with a teaser, a trailer of sorts, of the second book:

During our investigation, the night was utterly still until we had a moment that set all of our hearts racing. Steve and Tammy, standing in the center of the front, downstairs room, were sharing space with a pegboard and work bench full of construction tools and equipment. None of us had touched or gone near that area because we instinctively knew that the personal tools of a carpenter or painter or contractor are sacred. But, as it happened, the spirits at Chastain House weren't so courteous.

BAM!

The loud noise caused all of us to jump.

In the dark, I heard Steve shout, "Shit!"

"What was that?!" I hollered amidst the exclamations of the rest of the team.

"I have no idea!" he exclaimed.

After much fumbling with flashlights and everyone gathering around Steve and Tammy, all of our hearts racing, we discovered that a handsaw, which had been hanging on the pegboard along the front wall of the room, was now on the floor. But, it wasn't at the base of the pegboard. Instead, it was on the floor several feet away from the pegboard.

Now, zoom in on our faces, one at a time, each with mouth dropped wide open...and, hold on to your EMF meters!

HEATHER DOBSON AND COMPANY
will return in
RECOLLECTIONS OF A FUTURE GHOST
Summer, 2020

For the scoop, follow Heather:
Facebook & Instagram @a.future.ghost
Twitter @afutureghosthsd
Website http://afutureghost.com

THANKSGIVING

HEY! YOU!

Yeah, I'm talking to *you!* The person who forked out dough to read this book, stuck through it all the way to the end, only to find an acknowledgements section named after a holiday. I chose "Thanksgiving" instead because I want to give thanks for all the people who helped make this book possible. Plus, next to Halloween, Thanksgiving is my favorite holiday. There's turkey, stuffing, green bean casserole, family drama, and the best part is, of course, the pumpkin pie! Unfortunately, many people tend to skim past this section of the book because they're all, "Yada, yada, I'm not in here so why do I care?" Trust me, hon. You're in here! If you stick through to the end, you'll see!

In no particular order, here goes...

I want to profusely thank my editor, Wayne South Smith. I am the luckiest writer in the world to have him. Prior to this book's publication, we had never met face-to-face, but that didn't seem to matter because he and I just... clicked. Even though our communication has consisted solely of emails, phone calls, and written conversations within the process of working on the manuscript, we found this amazing rapport. His edits didn't just consist of "delete this, add this, put in a different word here." He pushed me, constantly, to become more than just a blogger who decided to write a bunch of disconnected posts on paper. He showed me that I could be a writer. Actually, no, scratch that. He pushed me to become an *author*. This book became more than what I had envisioned, and I have him to thank for that. He joked with me, laughed, cajoled, explained, and we had entire conversations about our lives, loves, and preferences, all in the comments pane of our writing software. He has constantly encouraged me to be a better writer, and it's because of this wonderful trust and friendship that this, my first book, is so very amazing. He made sure this book is something I can be proud of, and I can never repay him enough for that!

I am grateful to Sheryl Parbhoo for introducing me to my editor Wayne. I also want to thank her because pushed me to write this book without really knowing that she did it. She showed me that it was possible to raise kids and be an author. She probably doesn't remember it, but it was a few years back when we passed each other on the sidewalk during our morning runs/walks, and she happened to mention that she was writing her first book. Internally, my jaw dropped. *How on Earth is she raising five kids* and *writing a book?* I stewed on that all day long and realized that if she could find the time to write, so could I. I watched her go through the process of writing and publishing *The Unexpected Daughter*—an amazing book that you can buy at sherylparbhoo.com—and I couldn't be more proud of her! Many thanks to Sheryl for all of her advice, for pushing me when I hit walls, for checking in, and for sitting at the Starbucks for hours on end, writing together. As I finish this book, she is knee deep in her second. I need to catch up!

I cannot express enough gratitude to Larry Flaxman for writing the amazing foreword. As I reached the end of my writing, I knew I wanted someone from the paranormal field, who I respected and admired, to write an introduction, and his name immediately came to my mind. I have had the honor of listening to his lectures and investigating along-side him. His foreword brought tears to my eyes when I first read it, and it couldn't be more perfect. His books—that you can purchase at larryflaxman.com—have been an inspiration to me and many others in the paranormal field. Thank you!

I am so thankful for my friend and fellow taekwondo student, Paige Brigman. Not only is she a mom of three, wife, and black belt, she's also an amazing photographer! She was a natural choice to take my author headshot and cover photograph. My inspiration was the famous "lady in white" photograph taken at Bachelor's Grove Cemetery in Chicago. Through her camera and Photoshop mastery, Paige took the inspiration and artistically created an original photograph in a way I couldn't have imagined on my best day. I can't wait to see how she turns me into a ghost for my next two books. I know they will be as gorgeous as the photo on the cover of this book.

I'm so happy I chose Lindsay Starr as my cover deisgner. I sent her my specifications, wishes, ideas, and Paige's photos, and left her to it. Two weeks later, I literally cried when I saw my completed cover. She took a gorgeous photograph and turned it into something spooky and tangible I can hold in my hands, and a cover that will attract my readers. Lindsay made my dream come true. Thank you, L*!

My heartfelt appreciation to Jera Publishing for the interior design, making my words beautiful and even turning my chapter headings into mini-headstones with winged death standing sentinel as a silent reminder of our own impending demise. Thanks to Kimberly Martin, Stephanie Anderson, and everyone at Jera Publishing for making sure my book is itself a Memento Mori.

I want to give many thanks to my dear friend, Teri Sammons. When I told her that I wanted her to edit the early draft of my book to make sure I hadn't made any huge mistakes before sending it off to someone else, she took time outside her full-time job as an instructional designer to read through individual chapters and make suggestions. She told me many times, "Back off the thesaurus, woman!" which forced me to not be such a word-snob. A little bit of you is in this book, too, which makes it very special to me.

My PGI team is my family. They all know my deepest fears and secrets. We've cried together, been to each others' weddings, cradled new babies, and held each other when marriages failed. We sit around together in the dark and talk to the dead and to one another with absolute trust.

Clint Brownlee has pushed me to be a better investigator, mom, and person. He is always honest with me, he listens to me complain about stay-at-home-mom stuff, and he encourages me. He's an incredible person and has taught me so very much about life and investigating. He is such an inspiration and great friend!

Jordan Duncan is my homie. He makes me laugh, keeps me grounded, and I'm privileged to call him family. Love me some, J-Walk!

Stefanie Forte is my spirit animal! She is the toughest broad I know. She inspires me to be more and to follow my dreams. I am so very honored to be part of Canton Historic Haunts and sharing the ghosts of Canton, Georgia, with the general public. By the way? Her shop, Junk Drunk Jones—www.junkdrunkjones.com—in downtown Canton, Georgia, is the perfect place to write, and I can't wait to go back and work on my second and third books!

Shawn Boettner, my brother, and Tammy Thomas, Steve Engelhard, Tommy Mancino, Nancy Capps, Jenny Brahm, Sherry Davenport, Matt Broderson, Jeremy Nichols, Tasha Capps, and Philip Wyatt all helped me write this book by inspiring me at each investigation and every meeting. Their constant encouragement, love, humor, and understanding make me a better person, and they all carry a special place within these pages and in my heart.

For my neighbor, Jodi Murphy, who watched me have a front yard meltdown a few years ago, who looked me in the eye, and said, "Sister, go out and do something for you. I can see that you're angry and depressed and stuck." I took those words to heart, and when she registered for graduate school, I knew it was time to do something for me and here it is! I thank her for sharing many glasses of moscato, her front stoop, and her ear.

For Toni Iacozza and Jennifer Garner, my sorority sisters who have watched this journey from the *very* beginning, they opened up their homes when I worried about demons, they encouraged me to follow my heart, and they gave me the best advice of any two women I've ever known. I love them both very much!

For Betty and Charley Dobson, the best in-laws any girl could ever hope for! I want to thank them for their unconditional love, encouragement, help, and support! Words can't adequately describe how much I love and appreciate them both!

Amelia, Heath, and Jarrod have been, and always will be, my sweet babies. This book is truly for them. They are my legacy. Someday, they will be able to open these pages and hear my voice, see my face, and remember the endless months when I wrote this book and did absolutely *no* laundry. I love them all *so, so* much. More than words can express. They hold my heart.

And to my dear husband, Tyler. He gets me. He completes me. He is my hero, my love, and my everything. We've been through thick and thin, and I am so thankful for him and his unconditional love. His unwavering support and belief in me and my abilities made this book possible. I want to thank him for absolutely everything. *Vous et nul autre.*

And here *YOU* are! Last, but certainly not least, I want to thank you, my dear reader. Maybe you're a friend of mine, a relative, a fellow alumni from college—*Delta Zeta Sorority Forever!*—or high school—Go *Black Eagles!* Maybe we've never met and you found this book through a Google search or Amazon. Who knows? The fact of the matter is that you took a chance on me, purchased this book, read it all the way to the end, and loved it. And I want to thank you so very much for doing that. YOU mean the world to me!

FUTURE OBITUARY OF HEATHER SCARBRO DOBSON

Heather Scarbro Dobson, 47, of Woodstock, Georgia, has not yet passed away. Someday, though, after a brief, or possibly long, illness, or maybe even after a horrible accident—like tripping over her own feet—she will move on from this mortal coil to whatever happens next.

Heather started out life as a scared, too-smart-for-her-own-good little girl in the town of Charleston, West Virginia, with a father who loved to tell her stories of the creatures and ghosts of her home state. Even though those tales fascinated her, she remained frightened of the unknown, and of the blank slate of death and eternity.

Eventually, Heather drove off into the wild, big world, got married, and started a family. Her husband knew of her fear of death and was able to help assuage it, but with the arrival of their three children, Heather became less afraid of her own inevitable death and more fearful of those of her children.

Rather than sit on her laurels, hoping for time to erase her anxiety, she joined a paranormal investigative group and began the journey of an after-lifetime. Her nights were soon filled with shadows, disembodied voices, cold chills, and even phantom touches. All too quickly, ten years passed and her fear had subsided, replaced with a respect for death and a knowledge that after her own certain end, she would go somewhere. And so would her loved ones. She had peace and wanted to share that with the world.

Thus, her book *Memoirs of a Future Ghost* was born. In it, she poured out her experiences with the paranormal, illustrating the very true, often funny, sometimes sad tales of her decade investigating ghosts and the people haunted by them. Her book became a love letter to science, life, and the afterlife. And she knew that it would help people across the country, and maybe even around the world, understand that death is nothing to be feared, that an afterlife exists, and that sometimes ghosts just miss their homes, their people, and their lives, and want to stay as close to all of it as they can.

Heather was a technical writer, a scuba diving instructor, and a volunteer at her children's schools. As a paranormal investigator with over eleven years of experience, she is well-equipped to meet the afterlife head-on. She is preceded in death by her grandfather, Simeon Berkley; her father, Thomas Scarbro; her uncles Curtis and Romie Scarbro; and her aunts Joy Jones and Allegra Daniel. She knows that they're out there, somewhere, in the great beyond, cheering her on.

In lieu of flowers, please consider reading her book and contributing to her second book fund. Condolences and praise can be sent to heather@afutureghost.com. Keep up with her to the very end on Facebook and Instagram @a.future.ghost, on Twitter @afutureghosthsd, and on her website http://afutureghost.com.

CPSIA information can be obtained
at www.ICGtesting.com
Printed in the USA
FSHW020651260719

9 781733 160100